Helion & Company Limited
Unit 8 Amherst Business Centre
Budbrooke Road
Warwick
CV34 5WE
England
Tel. 01926 499 619
Email: info@helion.co.uk
Website: www.helion.co.uk
Twitter: @helionbooks
Visit our blog http://blog.helion.co.uk/

Text © Steve Crump 2022
Colour artwork © Anderson Subtil, David Bocquelet, Luca Canossa, Tom Cooper 2022
Diagrams and maps © George Anderson and Tom Cooper 2022
Photographs © as individually credited

Designed & typeset by Farr out Publications, Wokingham, Berkshire
Cover design by Paul Hewitt, Battlefield Design (www.battlefield-design.co.uk)

Every reasonable effort has been made to trace copyright holders and to obtain their permission for the use of copyright material. The author and publisher apologise for any errors or omissions in this work, and would be grateful if notified of any corrections that should be incorporated in future reprints or editions of this book.

ISBN 978-1-915070-56-2

British Library Cataloguing-in-Publication Data
A catalogue record for this book is available from the British Library

All rights reserved. No part of this publication may be reproduced, stored in a retrieval system, or transmitted, in any form, or by any means, electronic, mechanical, photocopying, recording or otherwise, without the express written consent of Helion & Company Limited.

We always welcome receiving book proposals from prospective authors.

CONTENTS

Glossary		2
Acknowledgements		3
Preface		3
Introduction		4
1	The Road to War: The Ongulumbashe Raid and Formation of the OZ Guards	5
2	Transition from Home Guard to Ops K	14
3	Koevoet – The Early Days	16
4	Koevoet's Initial Doctrine and Tactics	21
5	1981 – Koevoet Expands	29
6	1982 – Operation Yahoo: Collaboration with the SADF	36
7	1983 – Koevoet Consolidates	39
8	1984 – The Lusaka Accord: Koevoet Stands Firm	46
Bibliography		57
Notes		57
About the Author		60

Note: In order to simplify the use of this book, all names, locations and geographic designations are as provided in *The Times World Atlas*, or other traditionally accepted major sources of reference, as of the time of described events. Correspondingly, the term 'Congo' designates the area of the former Belgian colony of the Congo Free State, granted independence as the Democratic Republic of the Congo in June 1960 and in use until 1971 when the country was renamed Republic of Zaire, which, in turn, reverted to Democratic Republic of the Congo in 1997, and which remains in use today. As such, Congo is not to be mistaken for the former French colony of Middle Congo (Moyen Congo), officially named the Republic of the Congo on its independence in August 1960, also known as Congo-Brazzaville.

Glossary

ANC	African National Congress
Blesbok	A mine-protected logistics variant of the Casspir
BSAP	British South Africa Police
call-sign	A deployable Koevoet capability that usually comprised four Casspir vehicles mounting 36 black trackers and nine white SAP officers; 45 in all
Caprivi	the territory that connects Namibia with Tanzania, often referred to as the 'Caprivi Strip'
Casspir	the iconic mine-protected vehicle utilised by Koevoet and as developed by the South African Council for Scientific and Industrial Research (CSIR) and the South African Police (SAP) – CASSPIR
COIN	Counter-Insurgency
cutline	the 50m-wide cleared strip that marked the Namibian and Angolan border. The cutline or 'yati' was aimed at allowing the South Africans to sight and track possible insurgent activity
FAPLA	*Forças Armadas para a Libertação de Angola* – the Angolan government's old, pre-election armed forces
FNLA	*Frente Nacional de Libertação de Angola* – one of the three nationalist groups that fought for independence in Angola
GPMG	General Purpose Machine Gun. The Belgian FN 7.62mm light machine gun frequently used by South African forces
HUMINT	Human Intelligence – the collection of information from human sources
IT	Information Teams. The initial intelligence gathering elements of Dreyer's Koevoet teams
Kaokoveld	the area to the west of Ovamboland. A mountainous desert that reaches out to the Atlantic coast
Kavango	the geography that is home to the Kavango tribe; east of Ovamboland and to the south of Angola
Koevoet	Afrikaans for 'crowbar'; otherwise known as 'Ops K' or the South West African Counter-Insurgency Unit (SWAPOLCOIN). After 1985, known as SWAPOL-TIN
Kraal	a village enclosure commonly found in Ovamboland. Families would set up a cluster of huts within a log embrasure
MPLA	*Movimento Popular de Libertação de Angola* (Popular Movement for the Liberation of Angola), now the governing party of the government of Angola
NAMPOL	Namibian Police Force
OAU	Organization of African Unity
operational area	the term given to the northern reaches of Namibia, bordering onto Angola and encompassing Kaokoveld (Sector 20), Ovamboland (Sector 10), the Kavango (Sector 70) and the Caprivi Strip
OPO	Ovambo People's Organisation
orbat	Order of battle
Oshakati	a Namibian town that was to become a large SADF operational centre and home to the headquarters of Koevoet
PATU	the Rhodesian Police Anti-Terrorist Unit
PLAN	People's Liberation Army of Namibia, the military wing of SWAPO during its nationalist struggle
POMZ	anti-personnel mine of Soviet origin, mounted on a stake and activated by a trip wire
R1	7.62mm Self Loading Rifle utilised by the SADF. Similar to the NATO 7.62mm Self Loading Rifle
R4	South African manufactured 5.56mm assault rifle based on the Israeli Galil rifle. This weapon saw extensive use with Koevoet as did its shorter barrelled version, the R5
RAR	Rhodesian African Rifles
RhSAS	Rhodesian Special Air Service
RLI	Rhodesian Light Infantry
RPD	7.62mm light machine gun of Soviet origin, popular with the insurgents
SAAF	South African Air Force
SADF	South African Defence Force, the apartheid-era South African army
SAMS	South African Medical Services
SAPS	South African Police Service
SAS	Special Air Service – the British special forces unit
SKS	a semi-automatic rifle of Soviet origin used by SWAPO
spoor	tracks left by SWAPO insurgents and PLAN fighters
STF	Special Task Force – an elite SAPS unit trained in counter-terrorism and counter-insurgency
SWANLA	South West African National Labour Association
SWAPO	South West Africa People's Organisation
SWAPOL	South West African Police
SWATF	South West African Territory Force – the, indigenous, apartheid-era Namibian army
TB	Temporary Base or 'Tydelike Basis' as referred to in Afrikaans
tracker	a Koevoet operator skilled in tracking SWAPO insurgents and PLAN fighters
UNITA	*União Nacional para a Independência Total de Angola* (National Union for the Total Independence of Angola), the opposition guerrilla force in Angola
Wolf Turbo	successor to the Casspir. An improved vehicle with an enhanced powerpack and better protection. Manufactured in Namibia by Windhoek Maschinen Fabrik (WMF)
ZANLA	Zimbabwe African National Liberation Army, the armed wing of ZANU during the Zimbabwean nationalist struggle
ZIPRA	Zimbabwe People's Revolutionary Army, the armed wing of ZAPU during the nationalist struggle

Acknowledgements

This two-volume work has been some undertaking and there are many I need to thank. In particular and very obviously, Jim Hooper for the use of his photographs, some of which are published here for the first time. Big thanks to Jim and to former Koevoet members Thinus Pretorius and Boesman Pretorius for their time spent reviewing and fact checking the manuscript. Thank you, too, to Mike Visagie formerly of call-sign Zulu Alpha for details of Koevoet training and call-sign deployments in the field. I need to also place on record my thanks to Francois du Toit and the late Sisingi Kamongo. Our conversations go way back to London in 2011, facilitated by the ever-resourceful Leon Bezuidenhout, where it was a real privilege to learn first-hand of the Koevoet experience; the reality as opposed to what is said to have happened by the revisionists, the armchair warriors and the academics. Shoutouts too, to Jonathan Pittaway for permission to quote from his immense work *Koevoet: The Men Speak* and Johan Schoeman, for permission to use call-sign graphics from his excellent *War in Angola* website.[1] Lastly, to team Helion – Duncan Rogers, Tom Cooper and Bill Norton. Much appreciated your support.

Steve Crump
Brighton, June 2022

Preface

In 1997, I was the Programme Co-ordinator for the Mines Advisory Group (MAG) Humanitarian Mine Action programme in Angola. Here, I worked in Moxico and Cunene Provinces to support Mine Action Teams (MATs) clearing the legacy of the Namibian War of Liberation; namely landmines and Unexploded Ordnance (UXO). This was fascinating work and immense in scale. Indeed, in the last decade and in partnership with the Angolan government, MAG has cleared 10 million square metres of minefields, enabling communities to rebuild their lives after conflict and to live safely and without fear of traumatic injury.

In addressing the challenge of post-conflict rehabilitation, MAG would proactively seek to employ former combatants in its MATs. This to foster the rebuilding of communities and to enable economic revival; putting money into the hands of those who, ordinarily, would not have been able to work and feed their families. Amongst the Cunene MATs, skilfully led by MAG's Technical Adviser, Mark Manning, I was to encounter former members of the South West African People's Organisation (SWAPO), former People's Liberation Army of Namibia (PLAN) fighters and those who had fought with the National Union for the Total Independence of Angola (UNITA) and the Popular Movement for the Liberation of Angola (MPLA). All had been brought together to clear the silent and hidden killers; the irony being that some of the individuals involved had laid the devices they were now clearing. Hence I was to learn of the Liberation War and the insurgency first-hand and to gain a unique perspective on the conflict. Having lived in South Africa for a short while, I had certainly heard the experiences and views of former white South African Defence Force (SADF) 'troepies', but this was different. The guerrillas, the comrades, the 'other side' and, seemingly, their collective fear of some South African counter-insurgency unit which they suggested had been especially effective.

In my role as a programme co-ordinator, I also supported MAG's Namibian assessment mission which saw MAG collaborate with the Explosives Inspectorate of the Namibian Police, to ascertain the potential for joint clearance work in northern Namibia. The SADF had used landmines during the war and the South African Air Force (SAAF) had deployed considerable amounts of air-dropped ordnance. The mines had been laid principally to protect military encampments and military installations, but also civil infrastructure such as power lines. SWAPO and PLAN fighters had also used landmines to protect weapon caches and to disrupt South African military operations, and they would also lay mines to spread fear and dislocation amongst the local population.

Through researching for the MAG assessment, I began to learn of 'Ops K' or Koevoet. This was the counter-insurgency unit I had heard mention of in Angola, but now for the first time I began to understand what Koevoet was and how it operated. Its reputation as a counter-insurgency (COIN) force was apparently second to none and its fighting record revered. Yet, it was also presented to me as a brutal killing machine that perpetrated the worst excesses of the apartheid regime. My research continued and over the years I was to meet a number of former Koevoet members – both white former policemen and black former trackers. Their stories fascinated and intrigued in equal measure, leading me to the author and photojournalist, Jim Hooper. Jim famously spent five months embedded with 'Ops K' at the height of the insurgency, the only journalist ever to do so. Twice wounded, he published his experiences in his best-selling work 'Koevoet!' Through one means and another, Jim and I were to collaborate on a rework and update of his classic which was to be republished in 2013 by Helion and GG Books: an imprint I set up for the purpose of releasing the updated version of Jim's book.

Koevoet continues to draw interest and attention, being described, variously, as 'one of modern history's most effective COIN units, with its success ascribed to the excellent tracking skills of black trackers'; to those who decry Koevoet, as apartheid South Africa's Waffen-SS. This two-volume Africa @War work will seek to examine the reality of Koevoet; to ascertain the true effectiveness of Ops K as a COIN capability and to determine the lessons learnt for future, global, COIN operations. Illustrated profusely and throughout with Jim Hooper's stunning photographs, some of which are published here for the first time, it is hoped that this study will be a useful addition to the Africa @War series.

Introduction

The South African Border War and the Namibian War of Liberation were two complex and convoluted occurrences that ran parallel to each other. In short, the Border War saw the South Africans trying to prevent the establishment of a Marxist state in Angola, whilst occupying Namibia, and the War of Liberation saw the nationalist liberation movement – the South West African People's Organisation (SWAPO) – mount an insurgency to remove the occupiers and establish an independent and sovereign Namibia. It requires concentrated effort to fully comprehend the intricacies of both conflicts with the student being confronted with an immense array of faction acronyms that confuse and challenge. The origins of both conflicts go back to the continental European 'Scramble for Africa' and are now becoming lost to time. Yet the preamble to the Border War and the liberation struggle was one of horror that saw the Germans exercise a ruthless genocide, forcing the movement of whole population groups and oppressing an entire geography, Namibia.

After the First World War and with the Germans defeated, the South Africans occupied Namibia – then known as South West Africa – seeing the territory as their own and it was here that the seeds for future conflict were sown. With the growth of African nationalism – and rightly so – it would only be a matter of time before political liberation movements would take up arms in pursuit of their respective ideological and nation state objectives, with Namibia and Zimbabwe being just two. What resulted in Namibia was a multi-dimensional war that was to last over 20 years, and which was to end in a stalemate; or compromise, dependent upon your view.

The Liberation War exhibited two key tracts. One being that of an indigenous-led effort to challenge the nightmare of South Africa's application of apartheid in Namibia and the other, an armed struggle to liberate Namibia, once and for all, from South Africa. The Liberation War took the form of an armed insurgency and the South Africans sought to counter this insurgency through a number of methods, including the deployment of specialised COIN units such as Koevoet.

At the request of Helion, these two volumes look to cover the context to the conflicts in a manner that is concise and engaging whilst tracing the development of Koevoet as a COIN capability. Volume 1 concentrates on Koevoet's origin, formation, and its operational employment to 1984; Volume 2 covers the period 1985 to 1989, documenting Koevoet's continued operational employment, and its role in the Nine Day War; this being the actions in April 1989 when a heavily armed SWAPO force sought to seize control of Namibia. Volume 2 also examines controversies and accusations against Koevoet, of which there were many.

It is trusted that these two volumes will provide the reader with an understanding of what constitutes an insurgency and how the lines between nationalistic liberation advocacy, armed insurrection and conventional warfare can become blurred, and the resultant maelstrom being fast moving and multi-dimensional, drawing in a wide range of civil society, liberation movement, policing and

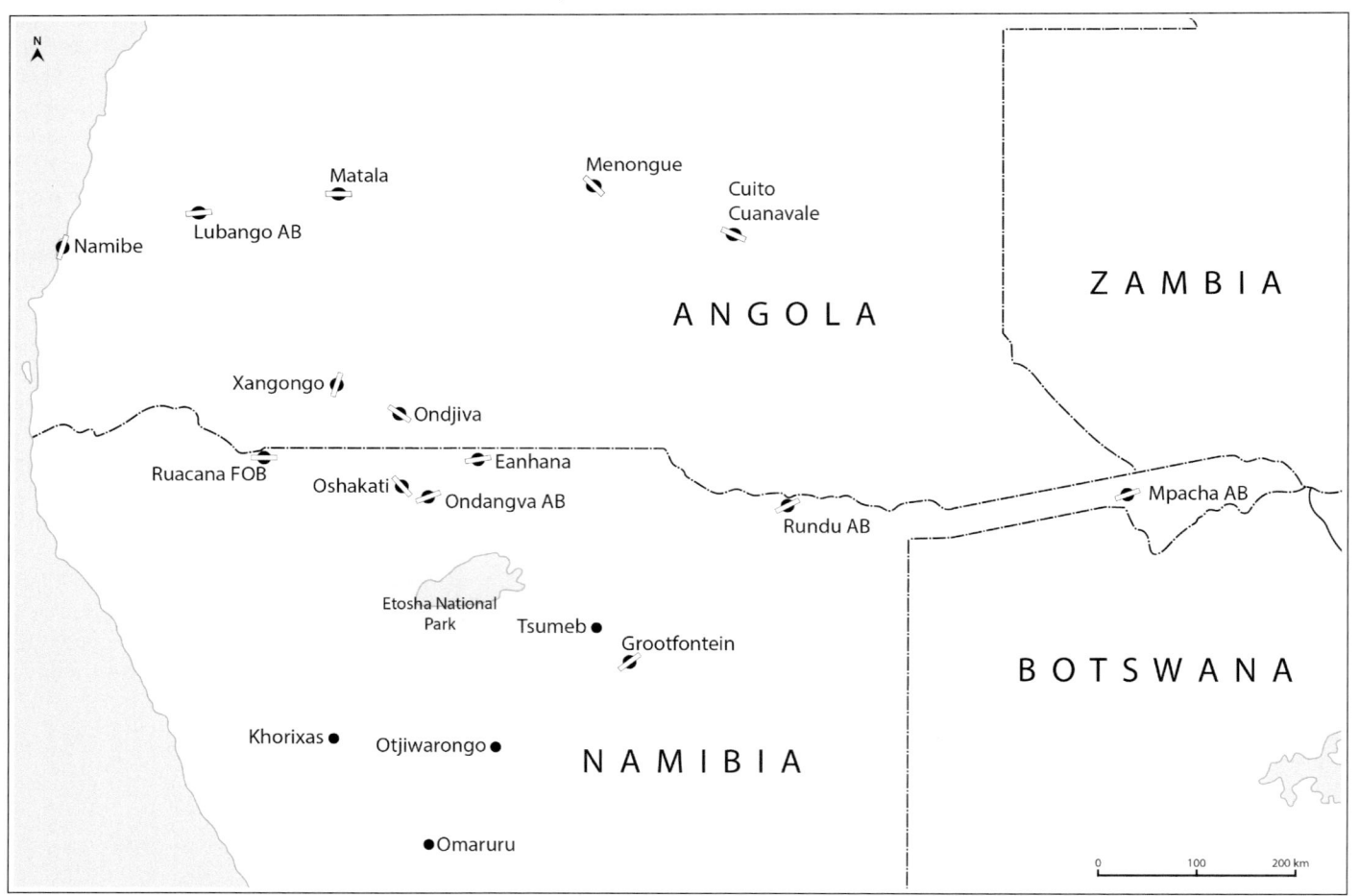

A map of southern Angola and northern South West Africa (nowadays Namibia), showing the most important airfields. (Map by George Anderson)

> ## Clarification: The complicated and often confusing relationship between the SAP and the SWAPOL
>
> Ops K, or Koevoet, was originally a South African Police (SAP) operation that was established by the Security Branch in Pretoria. Koevoet was initially very much part of the SAP. It drew its white police officer recruits from the SAP Security Branch, the SAP Special Task Force, and from a myriad of other SAP units. It also drew white recruits from the South West African Police (SWAPOL).
>
> SWAPOL was the national police force of Namibia, now known as the Namibian Police or NAMPOL. It was organised as a series of Directorates – for example, the Directorate of General Services, Directorate of Counter Insurgency, the Directorate of Crime Prevention and Investigations. It operated through a series of District Commands such as Rundu, Swakopmund and Oshakati. Thereafter, policing was delivered through a national network of police stations. SWAPOL was generally a white-officered force with black rank and file constables.
>
> In May 1985, Koevoet was amalgamated into the SWAPOL and technically became a SWAPOL responsibility, titled SWAPOL-TIN, though it was seen by many as very much as an SAP Security Branch property. Some members of the SAP were seconded to the SWAPOL to serve in the newly configured unit. When Koevoet was disbanded in 1989, its members were either reassigned to SWAPOL units or discharged from the service.

standing army participants. The role of intelligence is also examined and how Koevoet secured information through patrolling, arrests and interrogation. How does a COIN operation secure and utilise intelligence in pursuit of its objectives and how does this shape the resultant 'insurgency-space'? At the end of the day, any COIN force is only as effective as the men and women that serve in its ranks. Koevoet was certainly effective, uniquely integrating black and white into a mixed-race unit that demonstrated initiative, endeavour and proficiency.

Yet, during the Namibian War of Liberation, the activities of Koevoet were not well known. The unit professed a total distrust of the media and so deliberately sought to maintain a low profile in response to the frequent SWAPO accusations that Koevoet was conducting atrocities; occurrences which seemingly had many vocal witnesses to hand, always ready to discredit Koevoet and its commanders. That untoward incidents occurred is not disputed and atrocities certainly occurred but when Koevoet members transgressed the bounds of acceptability, they were invariably disciplined or handed over to the relevant authorities for due process. For those that did cross the accepted boundaries of law and responsibility, eventual accountability to the South African Truth and Reconciliation Commission awaited.

The Namibian War of Liberation was a hidden war. Unlike the Vietnam War, the Iran–Iraq War or the Falklands, it stayed out of the headlines. Few understood its intricacies, but the human cost was high. Many thousands killed and injured; many more displaced and dislocated. Whereas the chronological activities of the SADF during the war can be traced as a series of well documented operations, offensives and externals such as Op Protea, Op Daisy, Op Savannah and more, for Koevoet the critical path is less clear. Its operations were conducted as a regular and routine affair – seeking out intelligence, tracking down the insurgents, neutralising the enemy threat – day in and day out, week after week. For Koevoet, operational resilience and stamina, the wherewithal to keep going, was essential.

However, despite Koevoet's operational effectiveness and combat utility, it was to experience disbandment and demobilisation when in 1988, the South Africans withdrew from Angola and Namibia. In the Tripartite Accord brokered by the United States, Pretoria ceded to UN supervised elections which would eventually lead to a sovereign and independent Namibia. For Koevoet, this was the end though its legacy echoes and persists through to today.

Note on Terminology

Throughout the text, unless there is a specific reason to do so, South West Africa is referred to as Namibia and the 'South West African Border War', often shortened to the 'Border War' or the 'Bush War', is variously referred to as the 'Namibian War of Liberation' or the 'insurgency'.

1

The Road to War: The Ongulumbashe Raid and Formation of the OZ Guards

The origination and deployment of Ops K into the Namibian War of liberation has its beginnings in the colonial 'Scramble for Africa', the seismic consequences of the First World War and the geopolitical crisis that arose after the Second World War, and which was to go on to become known as the Cold War. In short, it was this sequential series of global movements and events that was to lead to the SAP establishing the COIN capability that was named 'Ops K' – Operation 'Crowbar' – or 'Koevoet' in Afrikaans.

Whilst the history of the South African Border War and the War of Liberation has been documented extensively, it is important to consider the geography and timeline of occurrences that led to the Ongulambashe incident in August 1966, a small action which is

Seen from the gun position of a Koevoet Wolf Turbo, the harsh terrain of the Kaokoveld was in dramatic contrast to the dense bushveld of Ovamboland 150 kilometres to the east. (Jim Hooper)

seen by many as the first significant clash of the Liberation War and where the foundations for Koevoet were laid.

Namibia is as vast arid country of some 850,000km², larger by a third than France and more than three times the size of the UK. It features the Namib desert to the west and the Kalahari in the east, separated by a central plateau that boasts the highest sand dunes in the world. The thin Caprivi Strip stretches along the Zambezi and onto the border with Zambia before touching Zimbabwe. The Etosha Pan, south of the Angolan border, is a lake fed by northern rivers which teems with wildlife during a three-month rainy season. For the remaining nine months it lies dry, salt encrusted, white and dusty. From the Etosha up northwards into southern Angola, the terrain is that of savannah grassland of which Koevoet was to become especially familiar. Namibia is permanently in drought but with the cold Benguela current sweeping up the 1,400km Atlantic Ocean coastline and the cold air hitting the dry air over the hinterland, lingering fog is common, a fog that sustains unique plant life such as the Welwitschia and the Kokerboom, hardy to the otherwise relentless sun.

Since time immemorial, Ovambos, San Bushmen hunter-gatherers and Nama pastoralists have etched out an existence in this harsh terrain. At some point they were joined by the Damara, also hunter-gatherers, and then in the sixteenth and seventeenth centuries by Bantu-speaking Herero pastoralists who settled in the central plateau. This was a diverse population that was to further see the addition of Kavangos, Caprivians and Tswanas. The lot of this indigenous mix was to change little until the mid-1870s when the Dorsland Trek saw Cape Afrikaner travellers settle to the north of the central plateau, into what was known as Damaraland. An edgy co-existence developed between the Afrikaner settlers, the Herero and Nama, but it was the 1885 Berlin Convention that unleashed the 'Scramble for Africa' and set Namibia on the road to a horrific genocide that was to frame liberation thinking for the years ahead. In 1886, German treaties negotiated with Portugal and Britain led to the delineation of the present international boundaries. In 1878 the British annexed the harbour at Walvis Bay and in 1883, to the south, the Germans secured 'rights' to what was to become the port City of Luderitz. In 1884 the Germans placed the territory under 'protection' and in October 1890, built Francois Fort on a height overseeing Windhoek. They then went on to acquire the Caprivi Strip from the British through the Heligoland-Zanzibar Treaty which saw the Germans cede their interest in Zanzibar and Heligoland in the North Sea, the island famously destroyed by the Allied bombing in 1945, so as to secure access to the Zambezi and other German East African territories. With their dominance over Namibia affirmed, the German colonial powers exercised an authoritarian rule over the indigenous peoples. Forcibly put to work as slaves, their lands confiscated and livestock stolen, the Herero and Nama were driven into collective poverty as German settlers took what was once theirs.

Tensions naturally grew and these came to a head in 1904 with, firstly, the Herero and then the Nama rebellions. Led by Samuel Maherero, the Herero rose up against the Germans to be joined by the Nama, led by Captain Hendrik Witbooi. This joint assembly massacred an approximate 100 Germans in Okanandja before the Germans retaliated in force, crushing the rebellion at Waterburg. There then followed four years of systemic genocide as the Germans drove the Herero, Nama and San into the Namib desert where some 100,000 died from starvation and dehydration. Many more were incarcerated in concentration camps where disease and abuse were rife. In central and southern Namibia, an approximate 60 percent of the indigenous peoples were killed with their remaining lands handed over to German and other European settlers.

With the outbreak of the First World War in 1914, the Germans launched a number of pre-emptive strikes to stave off the threat of South African military intervention, but these were largely ineffective. In July 1915, under the command of General's Jan Smuts and Louis Botha, the South Africans launched an offensive which saw the Germans capitulate and surrender. For the South Africans, the German surrender was a long overdue opportunity for them to annex Namibia into the Union. This move was rejected by the League of Nations and so the South Africans were forced to rule the territory under a League of Nations mandate. Whilst in political terms, the South Africans had failed to secure their desired fifth province, in practical terms, they went on to administer the territory as their own. The League of Nations mandate had been granted on the proviso that the South Africans would prepare the indigenous peoples for political self-determination. Suffice to say, this empowerment was never forthcoming, and the peoples of Namibia continued to experience oppressive, authoritarian, rule with ongoing land seizures and distributions mounted in favour of German and Afrikaner settlers. Gradually, the Herero found themselves largely confined to Ovamboland and the Nama forced into tribal reserves which were, later, to be designated homelands. Resentment simmered and the urge to resist grew.

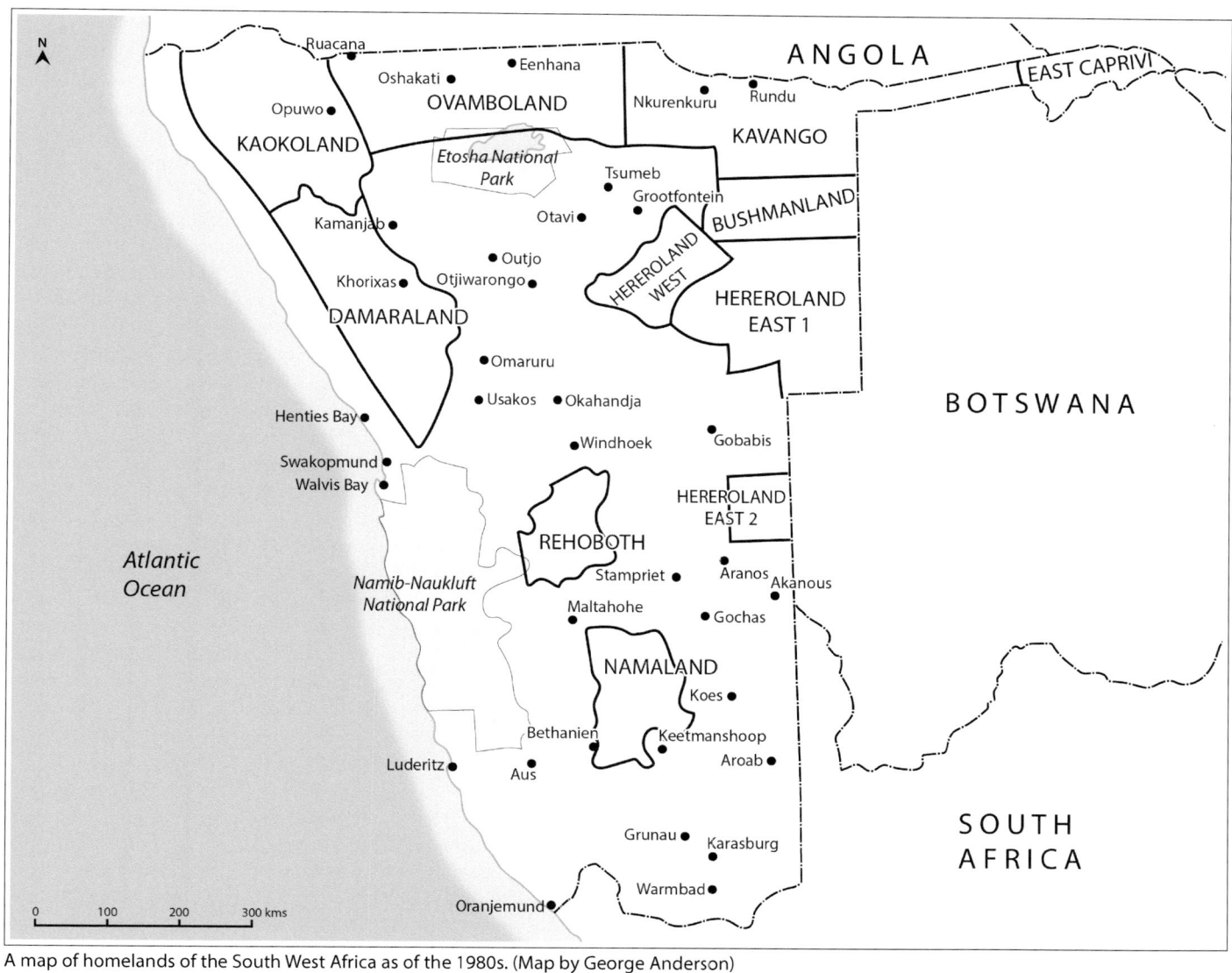

A map of homelands of the South West Africa as of the 1980s. (Map by George Anderson)

The Ovahimba people of the Kaokoveld, the north-westernmost province in Namibia – robust, resilient, and resourceful. (Jim Hooper)

During the Second World War, large-scale military action bypassed Namibia, but the South Africans used this time to consolidate their grip on the country and to continue their development of the civil society infrastructure that would enable them to govern 'their' province. In 1945, at the end of the Second World War and led by Smuts, they again sought to incorporate Namibia into the Union. Fearful of the secessionist movements that were gathering ground in Africa and central Asia, the newly established United Nations (UN) pushed back and rejected South Africa's demands. Yet with the demise of the League of Nations, the UN required South Africa to surrender its mandate to a UN trusteeship. South Africa rejected the UN's proposal and as might be expected, continued to treat Namibia as its own.

In 1948, the National Party's success at the polls saw DF Malan's newly formed government institute its policy of apartheid – or 'apartness.' Namibia fell under the jurisdiction of this codified system of racial segregation and black Namibians were subject to a raft of measures such as curfews and pass laws. This confined most of the indigenous peoples to designated homelands whilst opening up the rest of the country for 'development.' In a bold move aimed at solving the Namibian question once and for all, Malan's Nationalists withdrew from the UN mandate reporting programme and originated an electoral framework which saw the creation of new parliamentary seats. Under the very eyes of the UN and through the machination of supposed legitimate elections, South Africa finally acquired its fifth province. In uproar, the UN referred the matter to the International Court of Justice 'which ruled that Pretoria should continue its administration of the territory under the terms of the original mandate.'[1] South Africa continued to strengthen its grip on Namibia such that, in due course, its possession was absolute and total.

As diligently as the Nationalist government implemented the policy of apartheid in South Africa, in their newly acquired province, it was doubly applied with vim and vigour. With this came the beginnings of an organised resistance as industrialists – both foreign and South African – began to eye the extensive natural resources unique to Namibia. Off the coast, fishing stocks were abundant, commodities such as gold, diamonds and copper plentiful, land for herding livestock extensive. It was the indigenous population, confined to Ovamboland to the north and to tribal homelands in the east, west and upon the central plateau, which was to resource this rapid economic growth. Corralled into labour compounds, where the appalling conditions defied belief, black contract workers were subject to a regime that was both exploitative and dehumanising. Any minor infringement met with threats, violence and worse. 'Hired' through the government-run 'South West African Native Labour Association' (SWANLA), workers had no rights, no protection and no future. Condemned to a grinding existence which seemed to have no end, anger grew with the inevitable calls to resist.

All of this was occurring at a time when, globally, geopolitical tensions were rising. Whilst the United States and the Soviet Union had joined together to defeat Nazism, the alliance was never easy, and mistrust was present throughout. The Soviets were aggrieved at what they considered to be the late entry of the United States to the Second World War and the Americans were both wary and suspicious of Stalin, who they viewed as a tyrannical dictator responsible for brutalising millions.

These differences had been put aside in pursuit of victory over Nazi Germany, but only just. The relationship between the United States and the Soviet Union was wracked by scepticism and a mutual loathing. These sentiments were ever present at the Yalta Conference in February 1945 when the big three – Churchill, Roosevelt and Stalin – met to negotiate plans for what was expected to be post-war Europe. The conference was not without its challenges. Churchill was looking for free elections across Central and Eastern Europe, Roosevelt was seeking Soviet support for the newly established UN, and Stalin was labouring a strategic security policy for the Soviet Union that would see the development of a Central and Eastern European alliance of pro-communist nations. However, it was agreed that Germany would be divided into three occupation zones to be administered by the respective Allied nations. In addition, France – although not present at the conference – would administer a zone that was to be delineated within the proposed British and American zones. De Gaulle, the French President, affronted at the refusal of the big three to have him attend at Yalta, refused to accept the proposal and this 'French matter' was to become a notable pressure point for Churchill, Roosevelt and Stalin. Stalin was disdainful of France and was adamant that the French would play no role in the planned Allied Control Council or be a member of the Allied Reparations Committee. This was a tension, along with others, that was to resurface five months later in Potsdam.

With Germany now defeated, Churchill, Stalin and the newly incumbent President Truman – who had succeeded the US Presidency upon the death of Roosevelt – met again in July 1945 to confirm their plans for the post-war division of Germany. The meeting took place at the Cecilienhof Palace in Potsdam and as expected, was testy and difficult. The outcome was that Germany was to be divided into a West, to be administered by Britain, the United States and France (much to Stalin's disgust) and an East, which was to be administered by the Soviet Union. In the heart of communist East Germany lay the devastated city of Berlin, which was to be divided into four sectors each of which would be administered by one of the, supposed, wartime allies. This nervous arrangement persisted until 1948 when tension between the Western allies and the Soviets led to the Berlin Blockade. In protest at the allies' decision to introduce the West German Deutschmark to West Berlin, the Soviets blocked all routes into the city – air, road, canal and river. The resultant Berlin airlift lasted 231 days and left a deep mistrust that was compounded for the Soviets in 1949 when Truman engineered the foundation of the North Atlantic Treaty Organization (NATO).

NATO was seen as an immediate threat to the Soviets who, in response, moved quickly to establish the Warsaw Pact and to strengthen their influence across Eastern Europe; supporting fledgling pro-communist governments in East Germany, Poland, Hungary, Bulgaria, Czechoslovakia, Romania and Albania. Out of the ashes of the Second World War now emerged a new ideological, political, military and economic conflict, the Cold War, which was to see the United States and the Soviet Union, as nuclear armed states, vie for power and influence. Both the United States and the Soviet Union sought to build relationships with nation states in the global south whilst also supporting leaderships and movements that would be supportive of their respective ideologies; movements such as the resistance that was beginning to grow in Namibia.

In 1959, two activists, Sam Nujoma and Jacob Kuhangua, founded the Ovambo People's Organisation (OPO) in a move to crystallise resistance to SWANLA and its discriminatory labour law practices. Soon the OPO became more than a disruptive trade union of sorts but, rather, a wider political movement that looked to challenge apartheid and remove colonial rule. The work of the OPO became further defined when the South Africans attempted to move the entire population of Windhoek's 'Old Location' to a new settlement. The OPO along with the South West Africa National Union (SWANU) and the Chief's Council joined together under Nujoma's leadership to oppose this diktat and violent protests resulted. When the police opened fire on the protesters 'eleven rioters died and 54 were wounded.'[2] Nujoma fled to Tanzania where, headquartered in Dar es Salaam and effectively in exile, the OPO reconfigured itself as SWAPO with the talk amongst SWAPO's leadership increasingly of armed struggle. SWAPO's influence grew quickly, and the organisation enjoyed much popular support, but it was still failing to advocate its case at the UN. With the Soviet Union and other communist countries looking to grow their influence in sub-Saharan Africa, SWAPO found themselves with ready political, military and financial support. Empowered and emboldened, in 1962 SWAPO established a military wing, PLAN, that was charged to conduct offensive operations against the South Africans. PLAN was to be a 'volunteer' army that would wage a guerrilla insurgency in support of liberation. Recruited from across the tribal spectrum, the volunteers were initially trained in Algeria, Ghana and Egypt with a select few travelling to the Soviet Union. There, they received training in weapon handling, mine warfare, sabotage and the use of Improvised Explosive Devices (IEDs). This was accompanied for those in command and field leadership positions, by doctrinal training in Marxism and communist political theory. Over time, this training was to be augmented by the Chinese, Cubans and North Koreans who also supplied additional weaponry and munitions, whilst at the same time offering 'educational scholarships' to the SWAPO and PLAN volunteers. Scholarships meant attendance at a foreign training camp and subjugation to a harsh routine, where any dissenters or doubters were ruthlessly punished.

From 1965, PLAN was able to build up its forces as a steady flow of trained fighters began to assemble at its operational base in Tanzania. Granted to SWAPO by the Tanzanian government, with the full approval of the newly established Organization of African Unity (OAU) – whose 'Liberation Committee' recognised SWAPO as a legitimate liberation movement – Kongwa camp served as a training and accommodation facility. Later it was to grow in size and to play host to other such movements including South Africa's ANC and Zimbabwe's ZIPRA. But it was from Kongwa that six PLAN fighters moved into Ovamboland to set up satellite camps for the training of fighters. Five such camps, which also doubled as operational harbours, were established with one being at Ongulumbashe. To the west of Tsandi and hidden in the forest, the camp was laid out Soviet style with clearly marked defensive positions, accommodation shelters and storage bunkers.

Here, the former OPO activist, John ya Otto Nankudhu, began training local Ovambo's in the insurgent skills of small group tactics, weapon handling, ambush, sabotage and demolition. This alongside training in methods for the dissemination of liberation ideology and for the mobilisation of resistance.

The presence of PLAN fighters and of such a camp was difficult to keep secret and word began to circulate. Reports soon reached the SAP and the SAP Security Branch in Pretoria, who responded by setting up their own camp. Disguised as the field base for a civil engineering operation called PASCO, the facility enabled a small SAP team, led by Major Theunis Swanepoel (who was later to be labelled 'South Africa's chief interrogator') to move about the ground and to gather intelligence on the layout of the camp and the intentions of its occupants. Interestingly, the SAP team included a turned SWAPO informer, an indicator of what was to eventually become a standard Koevoet approach – the use of informers and turned fighters. Suffice to say, it did not take long for Swanepoel and his officers to locate and identify the PLAN camp at Ongulambashe.

In February 1966, a further 10 insurgents were deployed to join those in Ovamboland but en route through Angola, after they had robbed two Portuguese village stores and murdered their owners, they were intercepted near Rundu by the SAP from who they fled in disarray. The insurgents had sought to escape by splitting into two groups, but one group was captured along with a considerable array of documentation. During the subsequent interrogation, the SAP were able to confirm, both that PLAN fighters were operating in and around the Etosha Pan and that a training camp had, indeed, been sited at Ongulambashe.

It was now time for the SAP to strike and so under the command of SAP Brigadier Pat Dillon, an all-arms operation, titled Operation Blouwildebees, was to be mounted. This saw a small contingent of SADF Parabats (paratroopers), communication specialists, intelligence analysts and medics combine with SAP officers to form an assaulting force. The SADF contingent was commanded by the affable and mild-mannered paratrooper, Jan Breytenbach. A trained navigator and a veteran of the Royal Navy's Fleet Air Arm, Breytenbach was a career soldier who went onto establish 1 Reconnaissance Commando and the highly effective 32 Battalion.

Pictured whilst commanding the SADF's 44 Parachute Battalion, the renowned Jan Breytenbach, leaning against the vehicle's spare tyre, was to lead the Ongulambashe strike. (Graham Gillmore)

He was also to lead the SADF's Cassinga operation, known as Operation Reindeer which, in 1979, saw the largest operational parachute jump since the Second World War, with more than 800 South African Parabats jumping into and destroying a substantial PLAN camp.

To strike Ongulambashe, the joint force was hastily attired in SAP uniforms (the SADF were not at that time permitted to operate in Namibia and so had to move covertly) and moved to the SA Police College in Pretoria and its adjacent training area in Elandsfontein, where they rehearsed, and in some cases learnt from scratch, weapon handling, close quarter battle, helicopter and abseiling drills. Twenty-four men were readied for the operation with eight Alouette III helicopters of the SAAF placed on standby. Seven were to be used to convey the assault force and one was to act as the 'command car.' In order to disguise the operation as an SAP initiative, 'the helicopters of the SAAF had SAP badges painted on their fuselages, together with police serial numbers.'[3]

Following confirmatory reconnaissance of the Ongulambashe camp, which further evidenced the presence of PLAN insurgents, the assault was proposed for the early morning of 26 August. On 25 August, the assault force moved to the SAAF base in Ruacana from where the operation was to be mounted and where Pat Dillon assigned overall command of the operation to SAP Colonel Jan Blauw and to Major Swanepoel. This was to create tension as 'suggestions and inputs from the paratroopers were frequently overridden or ignored by the strong personalities amongst the police commanders.'[4]

This challenge withstanding, the final rehearsals saw the assault force broken down into six sticks of five men each assigned to one of the Alouette III helicopters. A mobile reserve force was assigned to Bedford 4-ton vehicles, and this was moved to the line of departure from which the assault would be launched. Armed with a combination of Uzi sub-machine guns and .303" Bren guns of Second World War vintage, and with Breytenbach as the Officer Commanding assaulting forces, the heliborne force established a forward operating base to the east of Ongulambashe and conducted last minute rehearsals ahead of the dawn assault. Breytenbach was now anxious to proceed, as the SAP were increasingly convinced that PLAN has been alerted to the raid by the local population who 'had become aware of the suspicious activities of the security policemen posing as civilians during the undercover operation.'[5]

The attack went in fast and immediately hit problems. Whilst on approach the helicopters came under fire and so the hasty decision was made to land the assault force rather than conduct an abseil insertion. The joint force was disembarked under continued fire with the command car orbiting above seeking to control the operation. On the ground, Breytenbach's men found themselves in a bunker complex which was seemingly abandoned, yet, onto which was directed the fire of some 20 or 30 alert fighters. Needing to win the firefight, they moved into infantry assault mode to clear the bunkers and sweep through the wider camp, this whilst the SAP trailed behind in confused disarray. Aloft, Blauw and Swanepoel called in the reserve force which was deployed in its 4-tonne Bedfords to secure the camp perimeter. In all, two insurgents were killed and nine were captured, with one prisoner presenting with serious gunshot wounds.

On having won the firefight and on securing the camp, the SAP retrieved an array of weapons, stores and documents. Later interrogation of the prisoners confirmed that one of the insurgents killed was a foreign-trained fighter. Furthermore, that PLAN had been preparing to launch offensive operations from Ongulambashe with the expectation that these would escalate, and lead to a state of war against the South Africans. It was clear to Pretoria that SWAPO were serious in their intent to destabilise and liberate Namibia and, on receiving the Minister of Police's report in parliament, that a 'terrorist' war had started. He urged the SAP to 'act against terrorists as if the country was at war.'[6]

For the SAP, Ongulambashe marked a line of departure and one that was to lead directly to the establishment of Koevoet. The SAP had only been able to mount the operation because of the support of the SADF and the SAAF. If the SAP were ever to successfully counter the infiltration of insurgents into Namibia, then much would need to change.

Namibia's vast geography was difficult to cover and police; 'the SAP was not prepared for guerrilla struggle in the north of Namibia.'[7] There were just 618 police officers deployed to the SAPS's 'South West Africa' Division where the concept of community policing, circa 1960s and in colonial sub-Saharan Africa, was barely defined, if at all. Consequently, 'intelligence' was lacking. If the SAP were on the back foot when it came to SWAPO and its political intentions, they were even more at a disadvantage when it came to PLAN with no experience, capability or appetite for a full-on COIN campaign.

Following the Ongulambashe raid, the SAP despatched reinforcements to northern Namibia. These officers were drawn from the SAP's riot police unit and they quickly found themselves engaged in a series of armed confrontations with SWAPO, one of which took place on the Zambezi when the SAP conducted a routine search of a passenger barge. The conducting officers surprised Tobias Hainyeko, a senior PLAN commander, who opened fire when he sought to make good his escape. Hainyeko 'leapt to his feet, drew a Tokarev pistol and shot (Warrant Officer Grobler) twice in the chest.'[8] He then went on to wound another police officer before he was shot dead himself.

This incident and a number of others prompted the despatch of further reinforcements and then, in June 1968, the commencement of formal training in 'COIN', as it was to be called by the SAP. Previously, the SAP has been archaic in its approach, deploying just white policeman who 'preferred search and destroy missions,'[9] as opposed to black officers with an understanding of the geography and civil society intricacies of the environment in which they were operating.

These early COIN courses were led by a joint SAP/SADF training team which oversaw and led the assembly of curriculum, methodology and practice, that drew reference from the SAP's extensive operational experience in Rhodesia – where the SAP were supporting operations against the Zimbabwe African National Union (ZANU) which, in turn, was being supported by the ANC. This COIN training was anchored in, and to, four key doctrinal perspectives.

A Focus on the ANC

The SAP actually saw the ANC as the premier threat to state security and was less concerned by SWAPO. As a result, its COIN doctrine and operational efforts were to be predominantly focused on countering the ANC, both, within the borders of South Africa and, externally, wherever the ANC had located its training bases and from where it was conducting insurgent operations. This including Tanzania, Zimbabwe and, less successfully, Zambia.

The Development of Doctrine

Heavily influenced by the ongoing experience of the Americans in Vietnam, South African COIN doctrine saw guerrilla insurgency as that mid-point between terrorism and fully-fledged conventional warfare. Consequently, the South Africans saw the aims and objectives of COIN as being the prevention of ad hoc terrorist acts so as to counter any transition to a low-level insurgency and, thereafter, to conventional warfighting. The role of the SAP and SADF was seen as preventing that transition to war.

Effective 'C3' – Command, Control & Coordination

The joint coordination of security forces, assets and intelligence was a key essential for success. Whilst both the SAP and SADF generally operated independently in Namibia, effective C3 was ensured through 'Joint Counter-Insurgency Committees.' These multi-agency committees allowed for the sharing of intelligence information and for the coordination of the joint policing and military warfighting response.

Secret Operations

That is, the mounting of secret offensive operations designed to disrupt and neutralise insurgent activity including, for example, pre-emptive strikes to destroy training bases, to kill insurgency leaders or disrupt supply chains. Secrecy around the state funding of COIN efforts, strategic alliances in support of COIN initiatives must remain secret – for example, international intelligence sharing or the execution of joint 'external' operations. In short, the more that was secret, the less the South Africans would need to explain.

These four perspectives were interwoven into the COIN theory training delivered at the SAP College at Pelindaba, just outside Pretoria, and into the practical courses that were held at the Malesoskop Farm in the Transvaal.

But just as the SAP worked to apply its new-found skills, SWAPO was ramping up its insurgent activity in Ovamboland and as far south as it could reach. The planting of landmines, the sabotage of civil society infrastructures, the rustling of livestock and the intimidation of the indigenous population continued, with the SAP seemingly powerless to address matters. It was essential that the insurgents be tracked and so the SAP worked to build a tracking capability which was drawn from members of the San Bushmen community and experienced national park rangers. With a known prowess for tracking, the Bushmen and rangers were mobilised as small tracking teams working out of camps sited, variously, along the border with Angola. Conducting routine patrols and often working with dogs, these teams would look for signs of insurgent activity and spoor; as in the Afrikaans word 'spoor', the scent and trail of a man or animal. Tracking as a skill was to become increasingly important to the SAP and, indeed was to be at the core of Koevoet's ways of working. With evidence of the British experience in Malaya, where Ibsan San trackers were deployed in support of the Special Air Service (SAS), and Rhodesia, where the British South Africa Police (BSAP) utilised tracker teams within its Police Anti-Terrorist Units (PATU), the South Africans developed a number of tracker training and continuation programmes. These included courses delivered within South Africa itself and out in the developing operational area.

Whether the spoor be a disturbed path, discarded food wrappings or accidently dropped ammunition, the SAP tracking teams would feed back this information to the SAP COIN elements who then proceed to mount the requisite follow-up action. As SWAPO and PLAN increased its attempts to infiltrate, the SAP stepped up its countermeasures, assembling 'Cobra Teams;' 'each consisting of five white personnel and one black Special Constable/interpreter, dropped into northern South West Africa for weeklong patrols to collect intelligence on SWAPO that reported to the SADF for action.'[10]

In addition to the Cobra Teams, the South Africans began to train and arm a number of militia and auxiliary bodies which were designed to support both the SADF and the SAP. One of these was the work of an enterprising SAP Security Branch Captain, George Steyn, who founded in 1974 what was to become known as the 'Ovambo Home Guard.'

In his Security Branch role and working as a liaison officer between the SAP and the SADF, Steyn was acutely aware of the need to monitor the border – or the 'yati' as it was called by the Ovambos or 'kaplyn' in Afrikaans – between Angola and Namibia. He saw the need to watch for SWAPO or PLAN incursions so that immediate and executive follow-up operations could be mounted. Steyn was especially keen to protect local community leaders from intimidation and, increasingly, assassination. Local government officials and community leaders were notable targets for SWAPO and assassination was rife.

Steyn's initiative saw the recruitment, training and deployment of a force of Special Constables that were to be known as 'Oscar Zulu' or 'OZ' guards. Most of these guards were San Bushmen from the kraals of the Kavango, Kaokoveld and Ovamboland. As before, these were experienced herders with an inherent and constitutional prowess for tracking; skills honed from birth as herders of livestock. A small number were Ovambos who had been assembled by the South Africans to disseminate political doctrine in school halls and 'shabeens' – illicit beer halls – where they would show propaganda films and hand out political pamphlets, gatherings that were surprisingly well attended.

Whilst initially this San Bushmen and Ovambo Home Guard was a relatively loose concern – the constables wore no uniform, were unpaid and were only lightly armed – Steyn could see the potential for developing a much more organised force, one which would play a real role in securing the intelligence vital for countering SWAPO. To this end, Steyn arranged for a small training team of black and white SAP officers to be based at Ohangwena where they were to train the Special Constables in basic guard force duties. One of the white police instructors was Sergeant Chris Nel. Nel had previously been involved in the training and deployment of the Cobra Teams. Occasionally these teams would be bolstered with the addition of a number of the OZ guards and as a result, Nel and Steyn had worked closely to share information and intelligence, building a situational analysis that was unrivalled at the time. Steyn was very much impressed with the Cobra Teams, and it was obvious to him that they were able to gather live, quality and ready information. Given such, he wasted no time in organising Nel's transfer to Ohangwena, which was some 14 kilometres south of the Angola border, so that they could work collectively to scale and deploy this new security asset.

At the beginning there were few weapons, no uniforms or any personal equipment for the OZ guards. Food was scarce and Steyn would have to victual his guard force through buying and bartering foodstuffs off local farmers, or through sequestrating ration stocks that had been 'written off' by the army quartermasters and which was augmented by bush meat hunted down by the Bushmen. He would 'drop off sacks of mealie meal, tinned food and so on.'[11]

Despite the limited resources, Steyn and Nel set about their training task with enthusiasm and a batch of 60 were put through a three-month training programme that, almost from the outset, went beyond the guard force brief. The recruits were trained in weapon handling, field craft (camouflage and concealment, judging distance etc.) and patrolling. They were also taught signalling skills

SWAPO insurgents and PLAN fighters were adept at caching weapons and explosives such as these POMZ anti-personnel mines and large Soviet TM-57, metal-cased anti-tank mines. These were often laid as 'reinforced mines' and were devastatingly effective. (Jim Hooper)

and that they 'turned out to be far better trackers' than the Bushmen.[12]

In 1978, Steyn's endeavour was formally constituted as the Ovambo Home Guard. This recognition acknowledged the real success of the OZ guards and served to affirm their value as a capable militia force, and one that was of real utility to the SADF. Now numbering some 3,000, the Ovambo Home Guard was attired in SADF browns and equipped with small arms; initially the German G3 and then the standard issue FN 7.62mm Self Loading Rifle, known in SADF parlance as the 'R1'. The very existence of the Home Guard presented a problem to SWAPO. Conversing with and observing local people going about their daily business, coupled with their familiarity with the local geography and terrain, the Ovambo Home Guard was able to build up a picture of activity along the cutline and the wider operational area. All of which enabled this guard force to be alert to any possible infiltration as SWAPO and PLAN sought to move people, weapons, explosives and other equipment into Namibia.

and combat first aid. Much of the training in patrolling, focused on the skills of reconnaissance and standing patrols, all critical if the Special Constables were to effectively identify and track SWAPO insurgents and PLAN fighters.

Once confirmed as 'fit for role', Steyn's OZ guards were deployed to conduct standalone border patrols, whereas a number were employed as trackers and interpreters, working alongside or embedded into SAP COIN teams and SADF units in the field. Others were used as static guards at security force bases. The guards were an immediate success and as a result, a further batch of 60 recruits, in this instance just Ovambos, were assembled for training. Nel found the Ovambos to be 'meticulous with personal hygiene'

It was routine for PLAN to bury arms in caches which they then protected with carefully laid anti-personnel mines. Disrupting the flow of weapons into Namibia and hampering their effective secretion was a priority for Steyn and his Home Guard, especially as PLAN fighters were limited in the amount of weapons and equipment they could carry and so access to a network of hidden caches was important. It was only through such means that SWAPO

Two Koevoet Wolf Turbos and a Casspir deployed along the 'cutline' or 'yati' – a 50m wide stretch of track that was cleared to assist the detection of insurgent activity, with footprints being readily apparent in the white sand. (Jim Hooper)

Clarification: Who is who and who is supporting/collaborating with whom?

The Namibian War of Liberation featured a number of actors. The mix is confusing and challenging to follow. In order to clarify matters and set out who was who, it is important to note that the principal protagonists were:

- SADF – The South African Defence Force
- SWATF – the South West African Territorial Force
- SAP – the South African Police
- SWAPOL – the South West African Police
- SWAPO – The South West African People's Organisation
- PLAN – People's Liberation Army of Namibia – SWAPO's fighting arm

The war ranged into Angola, what with the SADF 'externals' seeking to neutralise SWAPO and PLAN camps and training facilities located across the whole of southern Angola. This saw the principal protagonists come into contact with the Angolan movements to whom the Portuguese ceded power in 1974. These three movements failed to establish a joint and consensual coalition and hence a long civil war, within Angola, resulted.

So, whilst South Africa was countering the Namibian War of Liberation, it was also party to the Angolan civil war as it was backing UNITA. Conducting offensive operations against SWAPO and PLAN in Angola, saw the SADF in combat, variously, with FAPLA. FAPLA included the Angolan army and the Angolan air force.

The three Angolan pro-independence movements were:

MPLA – Popular Movement for the Liberation of Angola

The MPLA was founded in 1956 and was the result of a merger between two nationalist organisations. It was very much a Luanda-centric concern and was often in conflict with the FNLA and UNITA. It was, for all intents and purposes, the de facto government of Angola. Its armed element was titled FAPLA – the Popular Armed Forces for the Liberation of Angola. FAPLA was well organised and when operating with the Angolan air force, especially effective.

The MPLA and FAPLA were aligned to, and backed by, the Soviet Union, Cuba, China and North Korea. FAPLA forces were often deployed in support of SWAPO and PLAN.

FNLA – National Front for the Liberation of Angola

Largely a spent force by the time Dreyer established Koevoet, the FNLA was led by Roberto Holden and was backed by Zaire. It also drew covert support from the United States. The FNLA sought to secure Angolan independence from Portugal and thereafter, found itself fighting the MPLA and their Cuban backers. Roundly defeated during a series of actions in 1976, Holden was banished to Zaire, but the FNLA continued to fight on as the FNLA-COMIRA. It was eventually disbanded in 1983 with some of its former fighters being recruited into Koevoet and to Jan Breytenbach's 32 Battalion.

UNITA – The National Union for the Total Independence of Angola

UNITA was founded in 1966 and is today (2022) the second-largest political party in Angola. UNITA fought alongside the MPLA to secure independence from the Portuguese and then against the MPLA during the civil war that followed. Backed by the United States and the South Africans, UNITA's armed wing, the Armed Forces for the Liberation of Angola (FALA) performed well and success in the field led to the Cubans withdrawing several thousand troops. But when the Americans tired of supporting UNITA, they put pressure on its leader, Jonas Savimbi, to negotiate a ceasefire with the MPLA so as to allow free and fair elections. Eventually, through the Tripartite Agreement, a resolution was reached which saw the South African's withdraw and UNITA participate in the UN sponsored elections. These saw Savimbi defeated at the polls and the Angolan civil war resumed, only to meander on until 2002 when, following the death of Savimbi in an ambush, UNITA agreed a ceasefire with the MPLA government.

FALA – the Armed Forces for the Liberation of Angola

UNITA's armed wing – initially trained by the Chinese – FALA were effective against the Portuguese. In 1979, FALA comprised a number of 'regular' and 'territorial' units. This gave FALA the resilience to maintain insurgent and offensive operations right up to the elections in 1981 and through to UNITA's capitulation in 2002.

In summary, whilst Koevoet was operating to counter SWAPO and PLAN it sometimes, when pursuing insurgents into Angola or working alongside the SADF, found itself in combat with FAPLA.

The Angolan civil war took place alongside and during the Namibian War of Liberation – the two are intrinsically linked.

---

and PLAN would be able to build up the critical mass of weaponry essential for waging the insurgency.

Recognising that the guard force was now a credible force multiplier, the SADF moved to conduct joint, low-level, COIN operations with the Home Guard. This included the setting up of checkpoints, the execution of standing patrols and kraal sweeps. This enabled the Home Guard and the SAP to build up an intelligence picture through which they could address both civil criminality and the SWAPO insurgency. It also freed up the SADF so that its units could prosecute conventional warfighting against suspected or identified SWAPO insurgents and PLAN fighters on the border and, as was to become routine, in Angola itself. At a higher level, this Home Guard initiative enabled the South Africans to realise their desire to 'Namibianise' the war and to originate, develop and deploy a standalone military capability in Namibia. This to both reduce the perception that the conflict was an insurgency – but rather an internal civil conflict – and to also take the pressure off the already overstretched SADF.

For more than four years now, the SADF had been prosecuting offensive warfighting in Angola. The collapse of the colonial Portuguese government in 1974 as a result of Lisbon's 'Carnation Revolution' led to a political and power vacuum that saw all three of Angola's liberation movements pitted against each other in a vicious civil war where each sought to secure supremacy. The

South Africans watched in alarm as the National Liberation Front of Angola (FNLA), the MPLA and UNITA fought against each other, in what was to be the beginning of a relentless war that was to last some 40 years. By the time the MPLA achieved victory over UNITA in 2002, more than 800,000 people had been killed and the country left a shadow of its former self. But it was the arrival of Cuban military advisers in support of the MPLA that was to force the South Africans to act. There was a nervousness that the MPLA, along with the Cuban advisers, would bolster the strength and operational capability of PLAN who had now established themselves in southern Angola, where they believed they were beyond the reach of the SADF. Taken together, MPLA and PLAN proved a threat too far; one that the South Africans would have to counter through the discreet and tactical support of the FNLA and UNITA.

In October 1975 and with support from the Americans in the guise of CIA intelligence, the South Africans launched Operation Savannah. Reconnaissance (Recce) commando troops led by the ubiquitous Jan Breytenbach were embedded into FNLA and UNITA units and tasked to protect the Calueque Hydro-electric plant. Training teams were then deployed to upskill FNLA and UNITA so that they could better counter the MPLA threat. It was from these beginnings – and as so often happens with military interventions – that mission creep occurred. Operation Savannah was to last two years with more than 1,800 South African soldiers fielded in a number of combat groups. These groups fought alongside the FNLA and UNITA in an attempt to stabilise northern Angola and to stop the flow of Cuban troops and Soviet weaponry into the territory. By doing such, the South Africans were looking to strengthen FNLA and UNITA so that they could deny ground to SWAPO and prevent the incursion of SWAPO and PLAN fighters into Namibia.

However, Operation Savannah was to fail and despite South Africa's best efforts, Cuban forces continued to enter Angola. In December 1976, when a joint South African/FNLA action against the MPLA failed, the South Africans found themselves facing a stark reality. Having been outgunned and outnumbered, they realised that in order to continue to support FNLA and UNITA, they would need to reinforce their troops on the ground. But with a number of Western nations and some of the members of the Organization of African Unity (OAU) states teetering on recognising the MPLA as the legitimate power in Angola, this as a result of the 'Turnhalle talks' which were seeking a political resolution to the civil war and which proposed an interim government of settlement, the South Africans baulked and took the decision to withdraw. South Africa could not countenance a Marxist government in Angola and the presence of Cuban troops, but at the same time, they lacked the military resources and political will to sustain Operation Savannah.

An initiative which had once been shrouded in secrecy, had now become a very public debacle. In January 1976, South Africa withdrew to a line just north of the Angolan–Namibian border. Clearly this withdrawal emboldened SWAPO and PLAN who, with the tacit support of the MPLA regime in Luanda, went on to establish further camps and bases across southern Angola, from which they would then launch hit and run raids. With the insurgents able to melt back over the border and to the safety of their bases, the South Africans could only look on with alarm and frustration. But their response was bold and emphatic. So as 'to detect insurgent infiltration (they) removed around 50,000 people from Namibia's border with Angola and created a one-kilometre-wide depopulated strip or 'cutline' called the 'Yati.' Between the border and the white farming areas to the south, a network of sandy roads called 'cutlines' or 'kaplyne' were regularly swept by vehicles dragging trees and routinely patrolled for footprints.'[13]

But the South Africans would need to do more than just create a cutline and it was for this reason that the Home Guard was to play a key role in the establishment of Koevoet.

2
Transition from Home Guard to Ops K

As an 'external', Operation Savannah was one of a number of offensive operations the SADF was to mount into Angola during the course of the Liberation War, all which were conducted alongside the 'internal' COIN operations that were to be prosecuted by Koevoet. The failure of Operation Savannah was to have far reaching implications for an overstretched SADF, one that could not afford an increasing white 'body count', not to mention a growing number of conscripts returning home with life changing injuries. The SADF response was to overhaul its command structure and to raise a number of tribal units such as the 35 Ovambo Battalion, which was to eventually become '101 Battalion.' Originally tasked to deploy small tracking and interpreter teams in support of the regular SADF, 101 Battalion was to eventually be configured as a light infantry force not dissimilar to the Rhodesian Light Infantry (RLI). In time, 101 Battalion commanders were to be heavily influenced by the success of Koevoet and so the unit was to be rerolled as mechanised reaction forces or 'Romeo Mikes.' Indeed, 101 Battalion and Koevoet would regularly conduct joint mobile and reaction operations, frequently crossing into Angola on 'hot-pursuits.'

The SADF also raised the renowned 32 Battalion. Formed around a nucleus of former FNLA fighters, 32 was to become a force to be reckoned with. Elements were often deployed into Angola for weeks at a time, carrying out long range patrols aimed at identifying SWAPO and PLAN forces. Eventually, in August 1980, these diverse and multifaceted indigenous military capabilities would be drawn together into what was called the 'South West African Territory Force' (SWATF); a platform that was designed to 'form the basis for future SWA armed forces, around existing regional, Citizens Force and Commando units. By 1989, the SWATF provided some 70 percent of the ground forces deployed against SWAPO.'[1]

Despite the effort incurred in mounting Operation Savannah, SWAPO continued to infiltrate into Namibia and the OZ guards found themselves routinely deployed in support of SAP operations, whilst seeking to reassure an increasingly nervous civilian population. Steyn's concept was working well and in May 1978, its fortunes were to take a historic turn as a result of a chance encounter with a young and energetic police officer named Eugene de Kock.

From a staunch nationalist family, Eugene de Kock had first harboured military ambitions and initially sought to join the SADF.

Clarification: The Relationship between the South African Defence Force (SADF) and the South West Africa Territorial Force (SWATF)

The relationship between the SADF and the SWATF can be confusing and difficult to delineate. SWATF was essentially an auxiliary formation tasked to support the SADF. It was established in 1980 and drew its strength from the existing regular and territorial armed forces of South West Africa. The SWATF comprised a Permanent Force infantry unit, a logistic division, training elements and a territorial or Citizen Force component.

Initially, the SWATF's strength was around 10,000 men but by 1987 this had grown to 22,000 troops organised into tribal-centric Battalions such as 101 Battalion (Ovambo and Himba trackers), 201 (Bushmen Battalion), 701 Battalion (Kavangos). In addition, engineer, signals and a parachute Squadron were raised.

The SWATF was placed under the command of the Department of Defence for South West Africa and was led by an SADF general.

In practical terms, the SWATF was equipped and deployed as part of the SADF. Its Citizen Force reaction force – 91 Brigade – was equipped with the ubiquitous Ratel infantry fighting vehicle (IFV) and the Buffel.

The SWATF and the SADF were very much one and the same and joint operations were the norm. There was much cross-fertilisation such as the 101 Battalion and 1 ParaBat collaboration that originated the formation of the 1 SWA Specialist Unit. This was a reaction force capability that comprised a parachute trained, a short-lived horse-mounted element and motorcycle trackers. Formally transferred to the SWATF orbat in 1987, 1 SWA Specialist Unit was to enjoy considerable operational success.

But after just a year at the Army College in Pretoria, de Kock moved to join the SAP where early on 'it was clear he had ambition.'[2]

After completing his initial training and following a period of general police duties on the East Rand, de Kock was drafted to the SAP contingent assigned to support the Rhodesian PATU. Here, de Kock was to complete nine PATU tours patrolling the north-eastern border with Mozambique. Each lasting up to four months and working alongside the BSAP and the Rhodesian Army in small five/six man 'sticks', this PATU experience was to have a profound effect upon de Kock who, horrified by what he saw as the brutality of the Zimbabwe liberation movements' – ZIPRA and ZANLA – murderous efforts to intimidate the local population, made a firm personal commitment to countering terrorism in whatever way, shape or form he could.

One of the key architects of Koevoet – Eugene de Kock, pictured third from left, examines a captured RPG-75, a Soviet copy of the American LAW-72. (Jim Hooper)

Central to de Kock's thinking was the time he and his PATU colleagues spent with Rhodesian units such as the RLI, the Rhodesian African Rifles (RAR) and the Rhodesian Special Air Service (RhSAS). The all-white RLI – otherwise known as the 'Incredibles' – was a commando unit that prided itself on its first class fieldcraft skills. Through its 'Fireforce' platform, the RLI was to become a feared adversary and one that accounted for many terrorist, or 'terr', kills. The RAR was a black infantry unit with a white senior NCO and officer component. With the RAR, de Kock was impressed to see black and white soldiers deployed as an integrated force to conduct COIN operations. With regard to the RhSAS – formed out of the Rhodesian C Squadron that fought alongside the British in Malaya – de Kock observed that they 'were absolutely unconventional and worked in small or large groups dependent upon need and circumstances. But they lacked black members. In my view a combination of the two – the RAR and the RhSAS would be Africa's answer to terrorism.'[3]

The PATU experience and his exposure to the Rhodesian COIN shaped de Kock's developing perspectives on how to tackle the growing insurgency. This being small units and the integration of black and white into highly mobile ground assets supported by a dedicated aviation element – 'fireforce.' In addition, as proven by the Rhodesian Selous Scouts, to the use of covert and 'pseudo' groups that would infiltrate insurgent forces and prosecute unconventional acts to further the COIN mission.

In January 1977, as a rising star with the SAP, the newly promoted Lieutenant de Kock was posted to Ruacana police station as the 'Station Commander.' de Kock's express and deliberate intention was to experience station work and to become 'involved in counter-terrorism.'[4] A small town in the northern part of Namibia, Ruacana experienced considerable SWAPO and PLAN activity. Landmine strikes were common, intimidation and the murder of local officials rife. The SADF were taking casualties in the area and de Kock, as the senior SAP officer, would be the lead for the follow-up judicial investigations. This furthered de Kock's belief that new and dynamic ways of countering SWAPO needed to be found. In May 1978, de Kock was transferred out of Ruacana to Oshakati where he was to join the SAP Security Branch. There he was to encounter Steyn, Nel and their Ovambo Home Guard which he described as 'a joint project between the Security Branch of the SAP and the SADF. It aimed to make things difficult for SWAPO by keeping the human resources they needed out of their hands and serving as a resistance movement against them'. Whilst this unit had huge untapped potential, its commanding officer failed, sadly, to achieve its objective.'[5]

De Kock was critical of Steyn and Nel's methods, believing that the Home Guard could play a more proactive role in combatting SWAPO; and if there was ever a time to counter the insurgency it was now. In the 13 years since the Ongulumbashe action, much had changed. Once uncoordinated and confused, SWAPO was now, in 1979, infiltrating deep into Namibia, seemingly under the noses of the South Africans. The movement possessed a new vigour, a new ambition and it was demonstrating to the local population that it had the political and military means to challenge and overthrow the existing government. The differing tribal groups saw this and were increasingly aware that SWAPO was gaining confidence, influence and ground. 'And as with any insurgent war, it is the perceptions and sympathies of the population that determine ultimate victory or defeat.'[6]

For the people of Namibia, intimidation and assassination had become a daily feature. Landmine strikes were common, and the number of civilian deaths was increasing week by week. IEDs were set off in the capital Windhoek and in towns such as Swakopmund. SWAPO's developing confidence was such that it was laying ambushes in depth and was beginning to mount conventional infantry style attacks against the South African security forces as opposed to the classic hit and run, small scale, assaults it had sought to perfect over the years. All of this presented a huge challenge to the South Africans who were needing to demonstrate that they able to guarantee the human, personal and physical security of the local population, to protect and enhance their way of life. To deliver a stable state within which people could prosper and which would, ultimately, enable Pretoria to maintain the supposed political settlement which legitimised its fifth province.

De Kock was increasingly concerned that SWAPO was now operating unchecked; 'SWAPO insurgents – large groups of them at that – moved freely in Ovamboland. Guerrilla tactics dictate that you have the initiative, that you decide when you will act and how, and that you will not keep still. You keep moving. But on our side, a conventional warfare mindset prevailed, so the enemy could carry on enforcing its will. They went as far as declaring liberated zones.'[7]

This challenge had to be countered and so to deny ground to an increasingly belligerent SWAPO, Steyn, Nel and de Kock worked to increase the tempo of Ovambo Home Guard operations. Mounting frequent standing and roving patrols to reassure the population, to gather intelligence on SWAPO and when able to do so, to search, track and destroy the SWAPO insurgents and PLAN fighters. But early efforts were amateurish, with the patrols lacking effective coordination, firepower and mobility. Indeed, de Kock was himself lucky to survive a large ambush laid by 80 SWAPO fighters in which an Ovambo Special Constable was killed. His patrol was totally surprised by this SWAPO force which led to his Special Constables scattering in disarray; 'I managed to fire off one rifle grenade, but when I glanced to the left looking for the group I realised they had fled. There was no-one.'[8]

Finding himself alone, de Kock was forced to escape and evade capture by the insurgents. Over a two-day period, he moved across country to stay hidden, eventually flagging down a passing 4 x 4 that deposited him to safety. This was a salutary experience and one that was to confirm to de Kock that SWAPO was an able and aggressive adversary, one that simply had to be checked.

Yet it was to be elsewhere that de Kock was to apply the lessons learnt during this testing experience. In December 1979 de Kock and Nel were transferred to an all new and highly secret SAP unit that was named 'Ops K', and it was here that de Kock was to meet the visionary and indomitable Hans Dreyer.

3
Koevoet – The Early Days

It was Colonel 'Sterk' ('strong' in Afrikaans) Johannes (Hans) Dreyer of the SAP Security Branch who was to establish and lead Koevoet. Originally based in Port Elizabeth, he was tasked by the Commander of the SAP Security Branch, Lieutenant-General Johann Coetzee, 'to assist the SADF with information in their fight against SWAPO terrorists',[1] through the formation of a pseudo-ops unit that would consist of SADF Recce Commando operators and police officers from the SAP Security Branch. The unit was to be titled 'Ops K' or 'Koevoet' and its existence was classified.

With COIN experience from Mozambique, where he had observed the Portuguese 'Flechas' in action, and Rhodesia, where he had seen the Selous Scouts deployed to conduct pseudo operations against the liberation movements, ZIPRA and ZANLA, Dreyer sought to develop a semi-irregular capability, not dissimilar to the Scouts, that would secure, through investigative police work, information and intelligence on SWAPO and PLAN operations. This intelligence would then be collated and analysed, before being passed to the Recce Commandos of 5 Recce Regiment (whose insignia boasted a compass rose) who would then conduct the follow-up search and destroy operations. Central to Dreyer's thinking was the recruitment of 'turned' SWAPO fighters who would then be deployed against their former comrades in arms. With their 'lived' experience of SWAPO and their knowledge of how SWAPO and PLAN were organised, these Koevoet operators would be ideally placed to secure high quality intelligence. Through this means, Dreyer aimed to arrive at a joint SAP/SADF capability that would mutually reinforce and maximise. This alone was new and innovative thinking. Never had the SAP and SADF attempted to collaborate in such a way; to seek to

Hans Dreyer – attired in the all-green Koevoet uniform and canvas boots that were issued in early 1986. (Jim Hooper)

Dreyer led from the front; energetic and forceful, he was revered by the men of Koevoet, both black and white. (Jim Hooper)

conceive, plan and conduct joint operations that fused investigative police work with warfighting operations. Operations that would lead to the capture or neutralisation of SWAPO insurgents and PLAN fighters.

Dreyer's original intention was for Koevoet to 'source information and conduct interrogations, and for the Recce Commandos to be responsible for pseudo operations.'[2] This through the raising and deployment of a Koevoet led 'freedom force' that would advocate to the local population against SWAPO and conduct Recce commando sponsored 'black ops' that would 'infiltrate the freedom movement's territories and periodically attack the enemy. The group would also establish the enemy's positions and send them through to air and ground combat units for actions, poison their food and clothes.'[3] As time would tell, the reality would become something quite different.

To realise Coetzee's instruction, with the approval of both the SAP and SADF, Dreyer hand-picked four experienced Security Branch officers – Captain Andre Erwee, Captain Coetzee Els, Lieutenant 'Sakkie' du Plessis and Sergeant Willem Botha – and a number of SAP Special Task Force (STF) operatives, to accompany de Kock to Oshakati where 'Ops K' was to be based. Co-located with 5 Recce Regiment based at Fort Rev, adjacent to the Ondangwa Air Force base; 'the idea was that Koevoet (the SAP and the SADF Recce Commandos) would be involved in covert warfare. Koevoet had no special equipment or office furniture. The poor Security Branch officers did not even have chairs to sit on.'[4]

It was to this fledgling entity that de Kock and Nel were transferred and it was here that Dreyer and his small team commenced building an intelligence picture by reviewing all the archive data and information held by the Security Branch in Oshakati. This was a laborious process, but from this analysis, Dreyer's team was able to develop an intelligence assessment that detailed SWAPO's ways of working, its organisation, leadership and operational tactics. In addition, a database was assembled of known or suspected SWAPO insurgents and PLAN fighters operating in South West Africa. This information enabled Dreyer to develop a considered perspective on how SWAPO was operating and how best Koevoet could respond; where best the 'freedom force' might be deployed and, thereby, where pseudo operations might be conducted. This was essential given that Dreyer and his team had arrived 'cold', with little knowledge of the local area and they had received no welcoming or formal brief on the shape or form of insurgent activities to date.

It was clear that SWAPO were dominating the ground in Ovamboland and that the SAP were limited in their ability to act. Movement by road was at the risk of an ambush, movement cross-country at the risk of a landmine strike – and that was by day. There was no question that SWAPO owned the night. Overall, it was evident to Dreyer that SWAPO was operating at will and was looking to lay the foundations for a fully-fledged revolutionary war and one that, right under the gaze of the South Africans, would quickly transit from its current low-level intimidation, assassination and violence to a full insurgent offensive. Indeed, it appeared that SWAPO leaders were gearing for a full conventional war and their strategic planning reflected such: 'We created the eastern front covering eastern Caprivi and Kavango; the north-eastern front of eastern Ovamboland; and the north-western front of western Ovamboland and Kaooveld. All of these fronts had their own sectors, deep inside the country, within which PLAN combatants operated effectively.'[5]

In May 1979, Dreyer's team was small and had been working together for just five months – his core team comprised his four hand-picked Security Branch police officers and four experienced black SAP officers – two warrant officers; Dawid and Kandofi and two Sergeants; Kwagadi and Willicho, who had been tasked for translating and liaison work. To this, he added Nel and de Kock and a number of co-opted Ovambo Home Guards who would accompany his officers in a close protection capacity. To secure intelligence and to ascertain SWAPO's intentions, Dreyer needed to get his people out on the ground, moving across and within the local population, gathering critical information which would inform higher level planning and field operations. Koevoet needed to capture and interrogate SWAPO insurgents and PLAN fighters, but the quarry remained elusive. However, and as always is the case, a chance routine arrest led to a significant change in tempo.

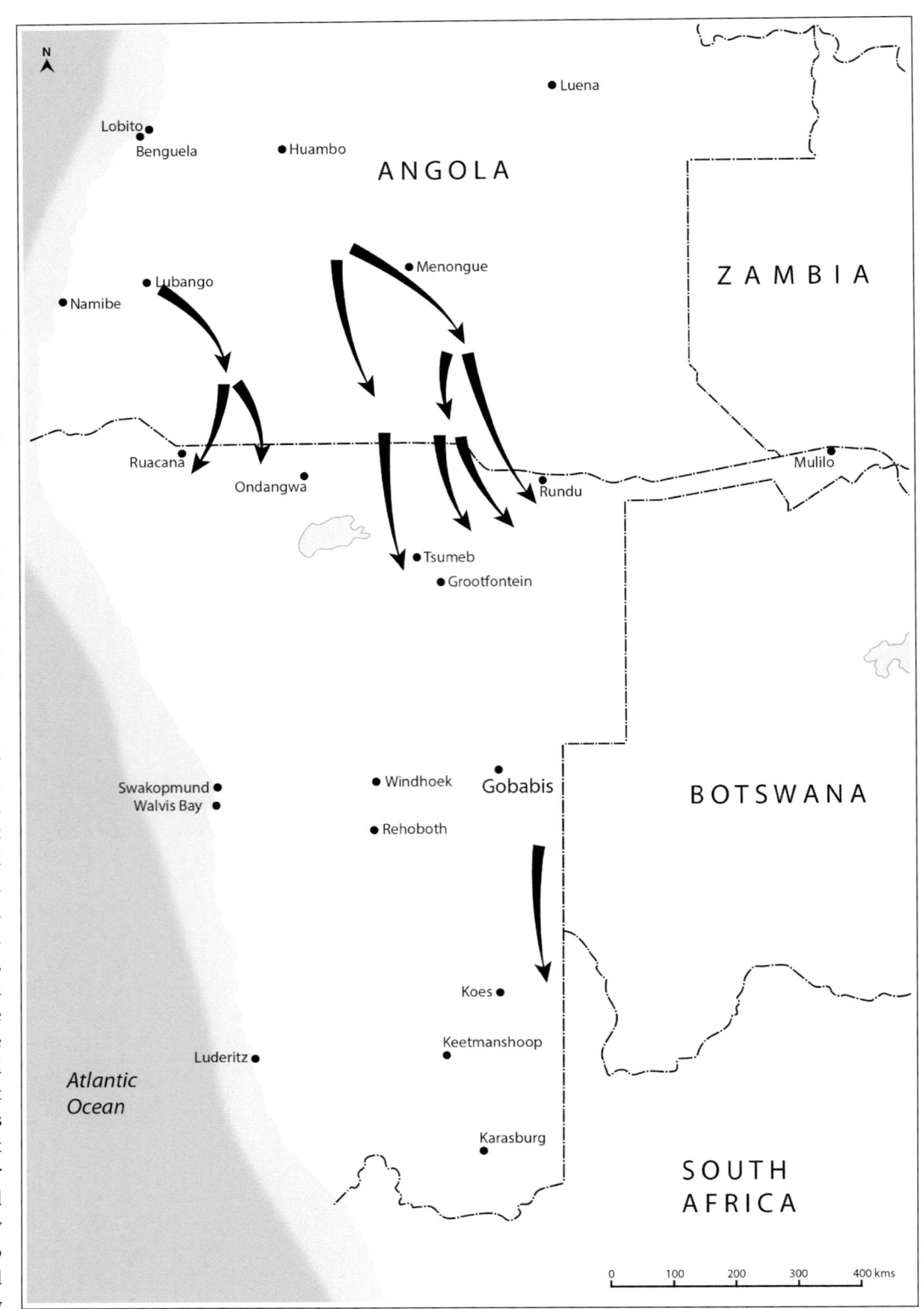

During a routine police patrol, Captain Els and Warrant Officer Dawid passed by a man riding a bicycle and wearing an unusual shirt, one that was not available locally. Els and Dawid challenged the individual who went to make an escape, dropping a pistol as he did so. They arrested the man who, under interrogation, was found to be a SWAPO intelligence officer tasked to sabotage power lines. He also divulged SWAPO's organisational layout in central Ovamboland – its numbers, strengths, equipment scales and more. This former insurgent was detained and immediately 'befriended' by Andre Erwee who 'began to drive around with the captured terrorist so that he could show us where the fellow travellers and other helpers lived.'[6] This

A map of major SWAPO infiltration routes into Namibia as of 1980. (Map by George Anderson)

remarkable occurrence led to a succession of arrests with those apprehended being held at the 5 Recce complex. From the subsequent interrogations, Dreyer and his men were able to update their initial intelligence assessment and further build their database of known or suspected SWAPO activists within Ovamboland, wider Namibia, and also wider afield in Angola. This included a specific lead that suggested that a group of some 90 insurgents had just infiltrated from the north into Ovamboland. This intelligence was presented to the SADF who assigned an elite Parachute Battalion (Parabat) to arrest and capture the insurgents. This operation was a success and Dreyer's men were able to conduct in-depth interrogations with a number of the captured insurgents. From the material secured Dreyer was able to enhance his intelligence assessments with ever-increasing detail. He was able to identify code names for the various insurgent leaders, their experiences, the location of likely arms caches, typical routes for infiltration and more.

Slowly Koevoet was beginning to take shape and the number of arrests increased daily. A number of those detained were 'given a choice to face legal action or join Koevoet.'[7] Experience was to show that these 'turned' insurgents would go on to be highly effective members of Koevoet.

But whilst Dreyer and his officers were beginning to secure valuable intelligence, there was also an increasing frustration that 5 Recce Regiment was slow to act on the leads provided and often, there was no follow-up. The relationship between Koevoet and the Recces began to deteriorate. The 5 Recce Regiment chain of command was happy for the Koevoet teams to investigate crime and gather intelligence, but they saw it as an army responsibility to mount follow-up and arrest operations. There was also a persistent tension and uncertainty around the role and composition of the Freedom Force and how the 5 Recce Regiment pseudo operations were to be conducted.

Speed was critical if the insurgents were to be countered and Dreyer was not one to linger. When insurgents mounted an infiltration into the farming district of Tsumeb and murdered a white grandmother and her two grandchildren, Dreyer mounted a vigorous follow-up. He tasked de Kock to lead the pursuit which saw a Koevoet team of 30, drawn mainly from the Ovambo Home Guard, track a SWAPO force of approximately 40 insurgents. In a series of sharp actions, de Kock's team was to rout and kill several of the insurgents. The follow-up was a success, but it also revealed some weaknesses – equipment scales needed addressing, signals equipment needed upgrading and voice procedures needed revision. But de Kock was positive as he observed; 'As in Rhodesia, I saw that combat teams made up of black and white soldiers – who were properly trained, were confident in the bush and had the latest technology – could be a winning recipe against SWAPO.'[8]

To improve the collaboration between Koevoet and 5 Recce Regiment, Dreyer drafted in a former police officer who was currently serving in the Recces as a 'go-between.' A veteran of the RhSAS, Frans Conradie was seen as the perfect liaison officer. He was duly transferred to the SAP and posted straight on to Koevoet where his work was to prove invaluable; he was both an exceptional liaison officer and a fearless leader in the field.

As Koevoet's intelligence picture evolved, Dreyer looked to consider how best his unit be deployed to counter the subversion, terrorism and armed insurrection that was developing as SWAPO's way of working. Given the uncertainty around the utility of the 'Freedom Force', he began to back away from 'the Selous Scouts idea, deciding that highly mobile and heavily armed hunter killer teams was the best way dealing with the insurgents.'[9]

Ever resourceful, Dreyer decided to take matters into his own hands and to strike out alone. He wanted to establish Koevoet as a standalone investigative and reactive capability. But to truly counter SWAPO's increasing threat and to realise Koevoet's potential, Dreyer needed human resource. Following discussions with de Kock it was to Nel that he turned. Aware that Nel had been central to the training and development of the Ovambo Home Guard, Dreyer suggested that some of the Special Constables be repurposed as a mobile capability that would investigate criminal activity, murder and sabotage. From the police intelligence secured and the leads generated, this mobile force would then conduct follow-up offensive operations aimed at seeking out, pursuing and neutralising the insurgents.

Dreyer ran his thinking pass George Steyn who was supportive and so without delay, Dreyer relocated Koevoet from the 5 Recce Regiment complex to what was called the 'White House' where Steyn was based. He then set about selecting 60 of the best Special Constables for training as Koevoet operatives. Priority was given to those who could speak either Afrikaans or English so that they would be able to converse with his white SAP officers. These 60 were sent on a basic combat skills course at the Wenela Camp in Ondangwa. This was delivered by SAP anti-terrorist STF officers, who had been attached to Koevoet on a three-month rotational tour, and covered basic infantry skills such as weapon handling, fieldcraft, and navigation. Upon completion, the recruits travelled to the Caprivi with Nel and de Kock to 'Fort Doppies, the Reconnaissance Commando's training base in the Caprivi for a month's intensive training.'[10] This further training covered advanced patrolling skills, tracking under fire and the laying of hasty ambushes.

This training was closely monitored by de Kock and Nel. Indeed, it was de Kock who 'was the first to suggest intense mobile infantry deployment drills for each and every Koevoet member: ordinary beat-walking or patrolling policemen became light, fast, mobile infantrymen.'[11]

Subsequent continuation training for the recruits and those that would follow, was conducted at a farm Dreyer secured for Koevoet's sole use and which was to be called Onaimwandi – named after a large tree that grew on the site. This unique facility was to serve as a headquarters, administrative office and training centre. It also included farm buildings and land, Dreyer's vision being that the farm would provide practical skills training – artisan skills, animal husbandry, small scale enterprise skills – that would enable his operatives to prepare for life after Koevoet. The farm also served as a leadership school. Dreyer placed great store on the development of leadership skills and was especially keen to identify operators who had the wherewithal and tenacity, to lead, when in testing conditions and under fire.

Located within what the South Africans called 'Sector 10' (in 1979, the operational area was divided into 10 sectors), much work was required to bring the farm up to the standard Dreyer required. Office buildings and barrack blocks had to be built alongside stores buildings, messes, detention cells and vehicle pounds. More than 6,000 hectares in size, 'captured SWAPO terrorists were accommodated at this base. It very much resembled an army barracks and was constructed from prefabricated board, corrugated iron sheets and beams which all fitted together like a lego set.'[12]

There was also the need to secure the weapons, vehicles, radios and other such stores equipment that Koevoet would require. Some was secured through the SAP chain of command. Other stores were 'liberated' from the SADF. There was much use of captured Soviet equipment including light arms, Rocket Propelled Grenades (RPGs), landmines and explosives. The unit's vehicle fleet was limited to just a small number of a 4 x 4 Ribboks, armoured landcruisers with dubious protective qualities, but this was soon to change.

With his recruits having now completed their training, Dreyer set about reorganising Koevoet. The attempts to establish the 'Freedom Force' and conduct pseudo operations had long been abandoned. Whilst a small group of Ovambo Special Constables had been deployed into the field to test the concept, it was obvious to Dreyer that infiltrating into SWAPO groups was no easy undertaking; 'In Ovamboland, SWAPO gangs had been resident for much longer and were more firmly established. They also had better communications with the Angolan bases and were better organised and informed. This made the infiltration of pseudo gangs riskier and far less successful.'[13]

Consequently, Dreyer reconfigured Koevoet to comprise a number of Investigative Teams (ITs) and reactive combat teams. De Kock and Conradie were to lead the first two combat teams, splitting the newly trained Special Constables equally between them and adding a number of former FNLA fighters and 'turned' SWAPO

The relationship between the SAAF and Koevoet was critical to its success; ever resilient, the SAAF helicopter pilots routinely carried out reconnaissance, fire-support and casevac missions in support of COIN operations. (Jim Hooper)

insurgents. De Kock's team took the call-sign 'Zulu Delta' and Conradie, 'Zulu Foxtrot'. 'Zulu' being the signals call-sign for the Koevoet HQ in Oshakati just as 'Zero' is utilised in today's NATO voice procedure as identification for the Commanding Officer or Headquarters station.

Early reactive work saw the combat teams deployed into Eastern Ovamboland by SAAF helicopter where they operated on foot to identify infiltration routes and the tracks of the individual insurgents. Given that the Ovambo Special Constables were familiar with the geography and terrain, success invariably occurred. Tracks or 'spoors' would be quickly identified, and the call-signs would mount a fast pursuit. With exceptional physical fitness and endurance, borne out of a childhood lived in the bush, the newly trained operatives were quickly able to close with their insurgent quarry. Once sighted, the pursuit would increase in tempo and lead to a firefight which would, inevitably, see the SWAPO insurgents and PLAN fighters neutralised.

Much was learned during this period and from the experience gained, de Kock and Conradie were able to shape thinking for the further and effective utilisation of Koevoet's combat teams. This including the need to move fast and light with a weapons mix that was easy to use at close quarters. Building upon the success generated by de Kock and Conradie, two other combat teams were established; Zulu Whiskey led by Sergeant Chris Wit and Zulu Sierra commanded by another sergeant, Pete Stassen.

In January 1980, Dreyer reported to Security Branch HQ in Pretoria that Koevoet now comprised an integrated, joint, investigative and reactive combat capability. The ITs were 'commanded by a Major with eight other officers and NCOs, fourteen black regular policemen and sixty Specials. They were divided into four teams to ensure they were strong enough to defend themselves in the event of an ambush' and four reactive fighting teams with 'eight white policemen, two regular black policemen and 308 Specials in total. They operated foot patrols from their Ongwadiva base where their administration and control was handled by a staff of two white and two black regular police officers. An additional white officer was temporarily attached to the joint police/army tactical command centre in Ongandjera.'[14]

Each IT and reactive combat team was equipped with a Hippo Mine Protected Vehicle (MPV) armed with either a 7.62mm FN MAG General Purpose Machine Gun or a 7.62mm MG-4 – these vehicles being 'the petrol engined and completely enclosed forerunner of the Casspir',[15] – and a Bedford 4-ton truck for the transport of logistic stores. The Hippos had been acquired against the odds by Dreyer in Pretoria, and yet the team leaders were originally reluctant to use them; 'I actually had to order the group leaders to take them. The first contact involving the Hippos resulted in eighteen dead insurgents. And that was with only two cars. After that everyone wanted them.'[16]

Now organised with a trained capability, equipped with functional weapon, equipment and vehicle scales, Koevoet was ready to counter SWAPO's insurgency as never before.

4
Koevoet's Initial Doctrine and Tactics

De Kock, Conradie, Stassen and Wit, as fighting team commanders, worked quickly to develop a set of operating principles and tactics that were aimed at maximising the COIN effectiveness of Koevoet. Dreyer's leadership style was to trust his commanders and vest in them the authority for setting the direction, coordination and control of Koevoet's assets and capabilities. His own experience from Mozambique and Rhodesia had taught him that COIN operations required that command be delegated to the lowest level and that both junior commanders and NCOs should be afforded the space to exercise the decision making they saw fit.

In broad terms, Dreyer's leadership developed Koevoet's operational doctrine around a broad four-part construct which was consigned to memory rather than be published as any formal doctrine per se. In essence, the construct comprised;

- The execution of investigative police work to secure intelligence from the community
- From intelligence secured, the identification of possible insurgent groups or activity, the advance to contact and the use of tracking skills to close with the enemy
- Upon contact, ascertaining the existence of insurgents, confirming their identity, numbers and strengths; search and destroy action to neutralise the insurgent threat
- Having won the action, re-organisation. Confirming numbers and identity of the dead, processing captives, securing intelligence and where appropriate thereafter, 'turning' insurgents to join Koevoet

The four separate elements of this construct were mutually reinforcing and ever dynamic. Indeed, a team might jump from the acquisition of intelligence straight to a search and destroy action; there was many an occasion when a surprised insurgent attempted to escape and evade when chanced upon a passing call-sign. This would lead to an immediate, executive and lethal response from Koevoet.

The construct applied to both the ITs and the combat teams and allowed for 'matrix working,' enabling the teams to work both 'vertically' (according to function) and 'horizontally' (according to the specific COIN requirement – that is evaluation of a possible spoor, the mounting of a pursuit or searching the dead for intelligence etc.). Working out in the community, visiting kraals, engaging with local headmen and other community leaders, the ITs would establish a Temporary Base (TB) from which they would work – conducting daily and overnight patrols out into the bush; indeed, there were times when the patrols would be out for weeks at a time. They would utilise police skills to investigate civil crime – such as livestock theft, family disputes – whilst also looking for signs of insurgent activity. If an insurgent spoor was spotted or a lead identified, the IT would then call in a reactive combat team who would 'advance to contact' through to, usually, a hot pursuit

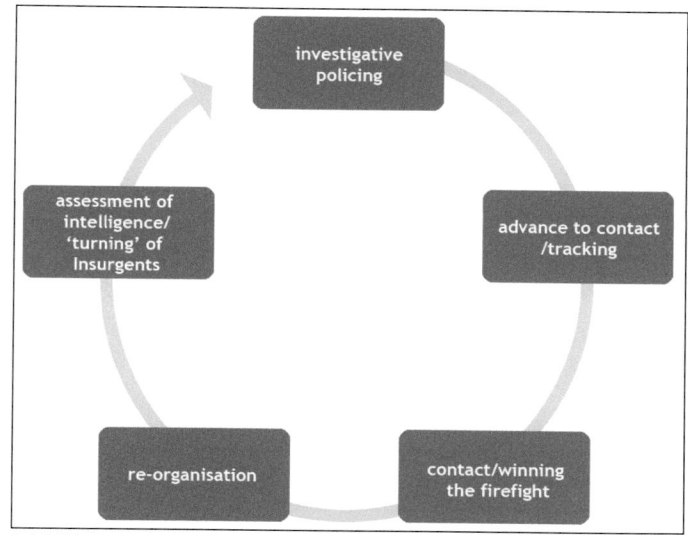

Initial Koevoet operating principals – the four-part construct. (Diagram by Tom Cooper)

and emphatic neutralisation of the threat. However, because of the time it might take a combat team to reach a specific grid reference or other such identified location, the IT would often have to conduct the pursuit itself, otherwise the SWAPO insurgent or PLAN fighter would be lost to contact and follow-up.

If a reactive combat team was tasked to pursuit, then it would use its Hippo MPV to move as quickly as possible to the location concerned to, then, pick up the spoor. Once the spoor had been identified and confirmed, trackers would be deployed onto the ground with the remainder of the team mounted in the vehicle. This gave the combat team the advantage of speed, mobility, firepower and protection. In addition, the Hippo could carry plentiful ammunition, water and rations should the pursuits become prolonged. The IT/combat team combination was to work well utilising the collective initiative of its junior commanders who took a flexible and matrix approach to joint working, but over time, the tempo of the insurgency and the need for immediate response led to the separate elements combining to become one joint and integrated call-sign.

Operational Planning

Alongside the four-point construct described, the exercise of command and manoeuvrability became central to Koevoet's approach to COIN. As previously mentioned, Dreyer encouraged junior commanders and, indeed, the Special Constables themselves to take the initiative, to exercise 'mission command.' Thinking trackers as opposed to those that had to be instructed what to do and when. This was very much demonstrated in the planning process when all members of the call-sign would work through a detailed planning process which broadly followed the sequence outlined below:

- The issue of mission orders
- Consultation with the call-sign team – 'How do we do this?' Best route in?'
- Preparation for pursuit – vehicles, fuel, weapon and ammunition checks
- Actions on – obstacles, mine strikes, ambush
- Execution – neutralisation of the SWAPO/PLAN threat
- Command & signals – with other call-signs, SAAF aviation assets, SADF vehicle recovery
- Recovery – management of captured insurgents, acquisition of intelligence

Whilst this detailed preparation might occur for a larger COIN activity perhaps in partnership with the SADF or the SAAF, Koevoet mission command often constituted the issue of quick battle orders with little or no chance to prepare weapons, equipment or rehearse 'actions on'. However, what with the Ovambo's local roots and their superb knowledge of the geography and terrain, the call-signs were usually able to move quickly onto a suspected spoor.

Right from the beginning, and especially after Dreyer instructed the separate IT and combat elements to combine, Koevoet was to excel and become masters of the 'manoeuvrist' approach. This being that approach to COIN operations where the requirement to neutralise the insurgent's cohesion and will to fight is uppermost, where junior commander initiative and original thinking is used to prosecute the offensive.

In looking to maximise Koevoet's ability to manoeuvre, Dreyer and his senior officers worked to evolve a joint, all-arms COIN-capability that made particular and distinct use of air assets. Initially this saw Dreyer's four combat teams call in SAAF assets – usually Alouette III or Puma helicopters – as and when they were required for spotting purposes or for casualty evacuation. But as Koevoet grew and its area of operations expanded, the Koevoet/SAAF partnership further developed, and the helicopter assets became an integral part of Koevoet's warfighting response. The SAAF performing a wide range of roles including tactical air reconnaissance, air transport (of specialists COIN assets such as SAP dogs and their handlers – or the execution of Koevoet 'eagle patrols' to mount snap roadblocks or to lay hasty ambushes) and close air support, which saw Alouette III gunships utilised to direct fire onto the insurgents or their positions.

In addition to the SAAF, Koevoet also utilised expertise from other parts of the SAP, the SWAPOL and the SADF. Officers from the SAP anti-terrorist STF were part of Koevoet right from the beginning at the Fort Doppies training centre. They were to work with Koevoet throughout its existence and were frequently deployed on operations. The SADF was to provide medical officers from the South African Medical Service (SAMS) and occasionally, elements from the Recce Commandos and other specialist SADF units would deploy with the Koevoet call-signs. Joint/parallel operations with 101 Battalion were common and the two units enjoyed a rivalry of sorts; 'If the army had something cooking, an intelligence officer from Koevoet's arch-rival, 101 Battalion, would be on hand for an additional briefing. Although a Koevoet group would happily chase spoor into an area where 101 was working, by tacit agreement they tended to avoid each other in the bush.'[1]

Through a process of organic evolution and considered practical application, Dreyer's Koevoet was, inadvertently, to be the architect of a modern approach to COIN that fused delegated command, manoeuvrability and 'all-arms' working into a high-tempo capability that was able to identify, track, close with and neutralise the insurgent threat.

From that point in January 1980 when Dreyer reported to Security Branch HQ that Koevoet was 'fit for role', the organisation continued to evolve and grow. As SWAPO increased its attempts to infiltrate into Ovamboland, Koevoet increased its capacity to respond. Call-signs were routinely added to Koevoet's 'Order of Battle' and new joiners from the SAP and the SWAPOL were arriving regularly to train the latest batch of Special Constable recruits. The training syllabus and programme, as originally developed by de Kock and Nel, was to last three months and took account of the fact that most of the Ovambos were illiterate;

Only relevant Koevoet material was presented after the initial disciplinary induction phase of about 6 weeks. Same weapons and equipment except radios as most Ovambos were completely illiterate. Remarkably, most taught themselves to read, write and numeric literacy to a degree where they could administer much of the team autonomously! Years after the war they would continue to astonish people not in the know with incredible skills and discipline on anti-crime operations in South Africa. Most Ovambos never had any formal schooling.[2]

This lack of formal education was echoed by Sisingi 'Shorty'

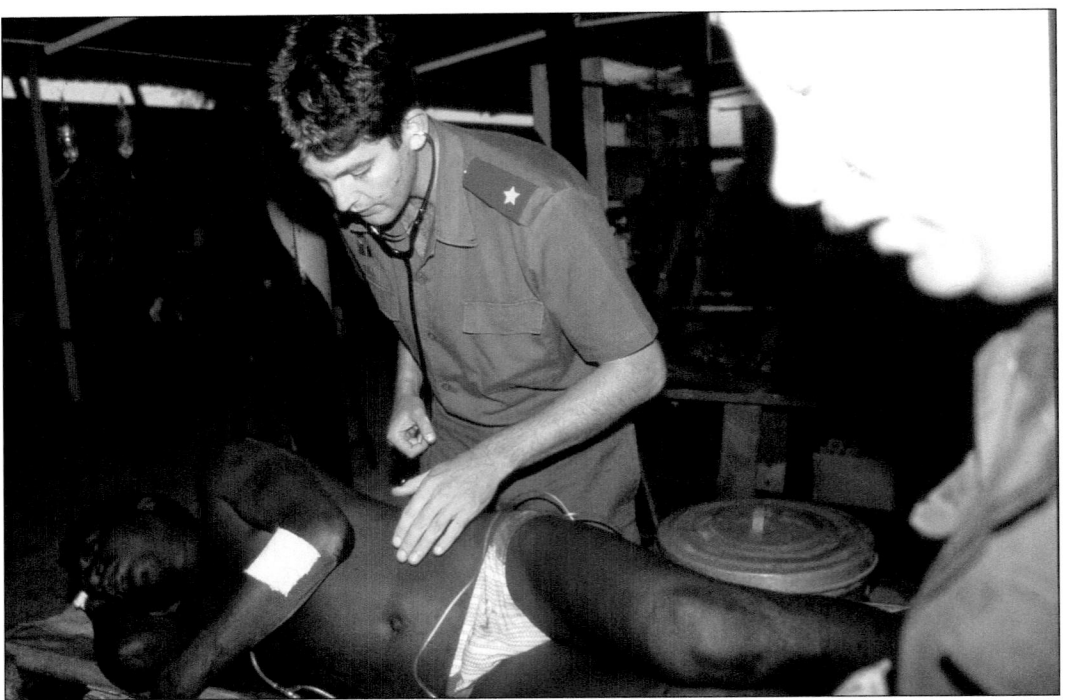

The South African Medical Service (SAMS) personnel assigned to Koevoet provided full and dedicated medical support to the call-signs. This including battlefield emergency and trauma care. This SAMS junior doctor treats a Koevoet member injured during a mortar strike on Koevoet's Ohangwena base. (Jim Hooper)

Ovambo trackers – team work was essential, with their local knowledge and their incredible physical fitness, the Ovambos could stay on a spoor for days. (Jim Hooper)

Kamongo, an Ovambo who joined Koevoet as a Special Constable and who went on to serve with distinction and attain the rank of sergeant; 'I grew up as a temporary cattle herder at Ndonga Omuramba in Kavangoland. In the afternoon after school, with no homework to be done, we had to care for the cattle. The herd was my grandfather's pride.'[3] Yet this herding of livestock was to lead to an incredible ability to read the land and to track:

> Finding a lost cow was always a challenge. But it would not always be animals: people also make tracks. We knew the difference between the tracks made by a woman and a man; we could differentiate between tracks made by a large woman and a small man. We could also tell the difference between the tracks made by a proud upright man and one less so. Everything by how one walks, how your foot makes contact with the earth. The tracks of an old person and those of a young one differ. We knew the differences. It was our way of living – a culture.[4]

This Ovambo experience, their culture and traditions as a people, was to lead to a social hierarchy within Koevoet that drew account of age, physical ability, mental aptitude and an individual's prowess for COIN operations. The Ovambos would propose new recruits themselves from amongst their families and kraals, suggesting those that they knew they could trust and work with.

But a lack of mobility was hampering Koevoet's ability to get out on the ground – the aging Ribboks and Hippos were more often 'off-road' than 'on-road' – and so in December 1980, Dreyer's Koevoet was to take delivery of three new Casspir Mine Protected Vehicles (MPVs). These were to be a significant multiplier for Koevoet, offering a mobility platform that had a dominating presence, which afforded light armoured protection to the call-signs and enabled the teams to mount devastating firepower. This in addition to the vehicles' load carrying capability which enabled the teams to be self-sufficient in rations, water and other stores. Crucial when out on the ground for any length of time.

Much has been written about the Casspir MPV but, in summary, the vehicle was developed out of collaboration between the SAP and South Africa's Council for Scientific Research (CSIR) – hence its name 'Casspir', an amalgamation of SAP and CSIR – and featured a unique 'V-bottom armoured monocoque hull design with the suspension modules located on the outside to ease repair and replacement.'[5]

An initial 190 Mark 1 Casspir vehicles were produced by Henred Fruehauf with the majority being utilised by the SAP. Further marks were developed and produced with Koevoet principally using the Mark 1 and Mark 2 before adopting the Wolf Turbo. In due course a number of Casspir variants were developed including the Blesbok logistics vehicle and the Duiker fuel bowser. These all exhibited the same Casspir characteristics; a 4x4 configuration, run-flat tyres (given that flat tyres were depressingly common), a high ground clearance and water-cooled diesel engines with 'the front of the vehicle is strengthened and optimised for bundu bashing.'[6]

The initial Koevoet reaction to the Casspir was derision; 'One was issued to Frans Conradie who used it for a week and disdainfully pronounced it useless. He believed a fighting vehicle should be open and the Casspir was closed in. It was also under-gunned having only a single 7.62mm light machine gun mounted on the front behind the cab.'[7]

However, from these inauspicious beginnings the Casspir was to become a formidable fighting platform. Dreyer's seniors added to its utility by simply angle grinding open the roof of the vehicle to allow for full and unobstructed 360-degree vision. They also worked to up-gun the weapon fit by adding brackets so that additional 7.62 FN MAG GPMG and .50-calibre Brownings could be added to the vehicle. In due course – and famously so – an enterprising team leader added an aircraft weapon system to his vehicle. Frans Conradie added a Mark 5 20mm Hispano-Suiza cannon surreptitiously acquired from contacts in the Rhodesian Air Force.

The key advantage of the Casspir was its survivability against IEDs. Any blast effect diminishes drastically with the distance from the detonation point. Thus, the high ground clearance of the Casspir, the spaced wheels and the hull shaped helped deflect the impact of the detonation. The Casspir certainly was not indestructible, Koevoet lost a number to RPG strikes and to HEAT STRIM impacts – a high explosive anti-tank rifle grenade of Yugoslavian origin – but it was as safe a platform as any other for the movement of call-signs across Namibia's arduous terrain.

As an increasing number of Casspirs were delivered to Koevoet, the unit became better able to tackle the SWAPO insurgency. In September 1981, Koevoet now had trained human resource (the ITs had now been rolled into the combat teams and an increasing number of 'turned' fighters had been integrated into the call-signs); weaponry (Koevoet was now scaled with the South African 5.56mm R5 rifle – light, dependable and rugged); a good informant network

Probably one of the most effective Mine Protected Vehicles (MPVs) of modern times, The Casspir was to provide Koevoet with an unrivalled mobility and firepower platform. This Zulu Uniform Casspir is equipped with 2 x 7.62mm MAG General Purpose Machine Guns (GPMG) and a .50-calibre Browning. A lethal combination. (Jim Hooper)

Two Casspirs cross a flooded chana during the Namibian rainy season. The suddenly abundant undergrowth would aid concealment of the insurgents and the frequent rains would wash away any trace of their movements. (Jim Hooper)

Ovamboland. This was always during the rainy season and follow-ups regularly occurred as far south as Otavia and even Otijwarongo.[8]

The rainy season, January to March, was to prove a real challenge for the Koevoet teams. The powdery, white, Namibian sand would turn to mud and the low lying chanas become waterlogged. A haven for mosquitos and a trap for the Casspirs which would often become bogged down. The rains would also make the identification of spoor impossible and many an insurgent was able to make their escape. Pursuing SWAPO during these incursions was highly dangerous and Koevoet was to take losses. The contacts would often be quick, intense and horrifyingly brutal with both black and white Koevoet officers killed, but as the teams became more experienced and the response to the insurgency evolve, tactics were refined and progressed.

The Koevoet Operational Sequence

Drawing reference from the doctrinal construct detailed earlier, Koevoet's tactics – that is the means by which its COIN capabilities were best utilised – centred on four warfighting functions. Namely, an integrated combination of lethal force, mobility, protection and shock action. By now, the Koevoet call-signs were operating as 'fighting groups' which were 'made up of four Casspirs, each with a team consisting of a team leader, driver, gunner and trackers.'[9] This gave the call-signs the scale with which to secure the tactical advantage over the insurgents.

The mounting and execution of Koevoet operations was soon to become an almost formulaic exercise. The sequence of activities being common across the Koevoet teams given that SADF procedures obviously had some influence on tactical ways of working, though call-sign leaders were allowed the flexibility to exercise their own leadership skills and judgements – for example, whether to conduct a baseline search for spoor or a fanline search. The following set of images, whilst drawn from a number of different actions, illustrate the typical application of Koevoet tactics. They have been placed in sequence to demonstrate what would be a routine patrol from its point of tasking to its return to base.

(the OZ Home Guard network/supportive community leaders); effective communications equipment (Koevoet was now equipped with base station and field radios); access to additional firepower assets (SAAF helicopters acting as gunships) and ready medical support in the form of embedded SAMS medics and doctors. But over and above the doctrinal four-part construct that shaped its operational employment, it was Koevoet's developing unit identity, aggression and culture that was to propel its success in the field where it was now encountering insurgent activity on an almost daily basis.

During the period 1981 to 1983, Dreyer's initial four call-signs increased to an approximate 20. This was barely enough to counter SWAPO insurgent and PLAN fighter activity;

> It was normal to chase ten to forty tracks anywhere in Ovamboland. In addition, the terrorists were still infiltrating to Rundu and trying to get down to Grootfontein. There was also an annual SWAPO Special Forces operation during which about 200 of SWAPO's best would try to infiltrate the farming areas south of

1. The Tasking

Most patrols would begin with a tasking, the delivery of briefings, the checking of weapons and equipment and the loading of stores; each combat team was divided into two groups – Alpha and Bravo – and these were rotated weekly. Whilst one group was operational – the other would be conducting routine maintenance or training.'[10] The maintenance of the Casspirs was an ongoing concern and there were many instances of modifications in the field; 'We had to build our own turrets for the machine guns, protection plates for the differentials, transfer case etc. and were constantly busy repairing Casspirs.'[11]

Ammunition and other stores are loaded onto the vehicles. The call-signs could sometimes be deployed out for weeks at a time. (Jim Hooper)

A Koevoet member checks his vehicle's 7.62mm Browning machine gun and .50-calibre Browning, co-axially mounted on a locally manufactured platform. (Jim Hooper)

A Koevoet team member questions a villager. (Jim Hooper)

There were occasions when the Koevoet teams would suspect that the local population had been harbouring SWAPO insurgents. It was common for SWAPO to force villagers to feed and house the insurgents but in some cases, the local population sided with the liberation movement and as such, were prepared to hide their presence from the South Africans. (Jim Hooper)

With the Casspirs nearby to afford mobility, Koevoet trackers pursue a spoor. The SWAPO insurgents and PLAN fighters were skilled at counter-tracking. (Jim Hooper)

Sensing they are close to the insurgents; the trackers break into a run. (Jim Hooper)

2. General Police Duties – The Gathering of Intelligence

Once out on the ground, the call-signs would conduct general duties policing activities, following up on recent intelligence leads or patrol their area of responsibility, engaging and questioning the civil population as to suspected SWAPO movements.

3. Acting on Intelligence – Identifying Tracks

Once an intelligence lead had been determined or a spoor identified, the tracker teams would deploy down from the Casspirs and look to pursue the insurgents.

Through their technical tracking skills and their sixth sense, the Koevoet trackers could quickly ascertain the number of insurgents they were pursuing, the amount of weapons and equipment they were carrying, and if any insurgents were injured. They had a 'natural fitness, agility and sixth sense. They could run for kilometres following the spoor.'[12] If availability permitted then SAAF air assets might be called in and the call-signs would be in communication with the helicopter or aircraft crew. Directions from the air would enable the trackers to further hone their advance on the insurgents. The size of the tracking team would be down to the call-sign commander's discretion given that there was a need to maintain focus; 'too many people on the ground take the focus away from the trackers and obscure the tracks. Having too many trackers on the ground is also dangerous for the Casspir drivers. If we hit a contact we have to be able to call upon the maximum firepower of the vehicle's machine guns.'[13]

4. The Pursuit

Knowing that they are being pursued, the insurgents might quickly bury weapons and

Shikongo Oholiko, one of call-sign Zulu Uniform's best trackers, leads on a spoor. (Jim Hooper)

An insurgent flees the Koevoet chase – outnumbered and outgunned. (Jim Hooper)

5. Winning the Firefight – Neutralising the Enemy

With Koevoet upon them, the SWAPO insurgents or the PLAN fighters would either fire and manoeuvre through the bush or go to ground. Some of the elite insurgent groups such as the 'Typhoon' units were especially well trained and superbly effective in the field. If numbers permitted, they would work in small teams of three and equipment, set hasty ambushes with anti-personnel mines such as the ubiquitous POMZ or split up into subgroups. The Casspirs would be called ahead to cut off the insurgents and lay down fire. Any air assets would also be brought in on target to lay additional suppressive fire. With the combination of vehicle mounted 7.62mm and .50-calibre guns and the trackers' R4 5.56mm personal weapons, it was possible for the call-signs to quickly generate lethal and devastating firepower, this being essential to prevent the insurgents fighting back. Equipped with Eastern-bloc weapons such as the RPG grenade launcher, the HEAT STRIM rifle grenade and the 7.62mm RPD machine gun, when cornered, the SWAPO insurgents and PLAN fighters could be a formidable and dangerous adversary.

With the open cabin, the Casspir provided the trackers with a high point from which to sight the enemy and from which to lay down suppressive and lethal fire. With the large rear doors, the trackers could disembark or re-enter the vehicle as they chose fit. This enabling a leapfrogging pursuit action to be conducted seamlessly. (Jim Hooper)

Aviation assets could be deployed to support the trackers – here an SAAF Alouette III is refuelled in the field. (Jim Hooper)

Seen from a Casspir, two vehicles bear down on an insurgent who has gone to ground in the undergrowth. The noise and the confusion of the action is evident with the air thick with dust and cordite. SWAPO were masters of the quick reaction and were every ready to fill capability gaps. Through teamwork and effective quick battle orders they were often able to mount an impressive and courageous defence which sometimes allowed them to make good their escape. (Jim Hooper)

the firefight, the tactical combination of mechanised mobility, armoured protection, lethal force and the shock of action – noise, weight of fire, use of smoke screens – invariably enabled the call-signs to neutralise and kill the insurgents.

The weapons used by the insurgents were simple, easy to use and even in the hands of a tired fighter, a significant threat to the Koevoet call-signs; 'One guerrilla was killed right away, but another knocked out a Zulu Tango Casspir with an anti-tank rifle grenade. The car caught fire but the crew baled out and there were no casualties.'[14]

With the combination of Koevoet's doctrinal construct and operational sequence described, Koevoet was able to effectively counter the SWAPO insurgency. With a ready flow of intelligence from its investigative policing, Dreyer's teams were able to pre-empt and predict; to deploy the teams where they were most likely to ensure a COIN economy of effort and resource, to achieve decisive results on a scale that justified the delegation of decision making to junior commanders. An approach that was central to Dreyer's overarching command philosophy and one that was to yield significant results as Koevoet continued to expand in size and operational reach.

The utility of the Casspir as a platform for COIN cannot be emphasised enough. The vehicle afforded car commanders a commanding view from which to direct operations and a weapons mount that could be easily augmented, adapted, and brought into action quickly. The signals-fit allowed for effective coordination across the call-sign, to base stations and, if required, the SAAF. (Jim Hooper)

Neutralised, the insurgent is searched for weapons, equipment and documentation. Pictured is call-sign Zulu Quebec's Francois du Toit removing explosive charges and ammunition from a dead insurgent. The body would then be retrieved to the Koeovet base for identification and disposal. Koevoet was adept at gathering and analysing intelligence. SWAPO's operational security could be poor, and notebooks, maps and plans were often found on captured and dead insurgents. These would yield a wealth of information as to SWAPO personalities and commanders, operational priorities, the location of weapon caches, known SWAPO sympathisers or opponents who were to be assassinated. This information would be collated and assessed to inform future Koevoet operations. Captured insurgents would be interrogated and where possible, 'turned' to join Koevoet. (Jim Hooper)

four to lay down defensive fire in depth. It was here that the tactic of using the Casspirs for mobility and protection came into its own. At height and with the armoured protection of the vehicles, the Koevoet teams could lay down suppressive fire whilst also using the bulk of the vehicle to intimidate and run down the enemy. In winning

5
1981 – Koevoet Expands

In 1981 Koeovet expanded its area of operations into Kaokoland to the west of Ovamboland and to and the Kavango, to the east, across to the Caprivi Strip and the area adjacent to the border with Angola and Botswana.

This was to counter the infiltration of SWAPO insurgents and PLAN's elite 'Typhoon' or 'Volcano' sabotage teams who were seeking to circuit Ovamboland, in their efforts to move south to attack the white residential and business areas of Arandis, Swakopmund and the capital Windhoek. Koevoet's efforts in Ovamboland were certainly hampering SWAPO's intentions and the tempo of operations was ferocious. These would typically peak during the rainy season which was to become known in due course as the 'annual summer games.'

> During the dry months, the insurgents would have to carry their water with them – an almost impossible task given the distance they had to walk – while SADF patrols would keep a close watch on water sources. During the rainy months, the vegetation was lush, giving excellent cover, while the muddy roads made it difficult for the South Africans to operate their vehicles.[1]

But with the launch of the SADF's 'external', 'Op Protea', into southern Angola, Koevoet was required to intensify its operations so as to intercept those insurgents who were continuing to infiltrate south.

Op Protea was aimed at challenging a recent build-up of SWAPO forces in southern Angola – on what SWAPO called its 'north-western front', where a number of training camps had been established. Protea was also aimed at dismantling the integrated air defence system – radar guided anti-aircraft guns and missile systems – that had been deployed by the Angolans to protect the SWAPO camps.

The action commenced in August with an SAAF air assault on the air defence infrastructure and a cross-border land intervention led by the SADF's premier mechanised formation, 61 Mech. This all-arms operation was executed with precision and saw SWAPO swept from Xangogo, Mongua and Ongiva. Koevoet teams were tasked to accompany the SADF elements and so crossed the border as part of this external. This was the first time Koevoet was knowingly deployed cross-border, but it certainly was not the first and would not be the last.

A key and emerging characteristic of Koevoet was that its call-sign leaders were given the latitude to pursue contacts as they saw fit; 'Koevoet was not bound by the company, battalion and sector boundaries of the military structure.'[2] Whilst a team would develop an intelligence picture and understanding of the specific area it was working in, Dreyer wanted Koevoet call-signs to be agile enough to cross into each other's area of operations as required and appropriate. This included, when necessary, pursuing SWAPO insurgents and PLAN fighters over the border and into Angola.

The requirement to be flexible was uppermost in Dreyer's mind when he established a Koevoet call-sign, Zulu 5 Sierra (Z5S), in Kaokoland. This team actually originated from an SAP Security Branch initiative which sought to replicate the success of Koevoet. An enterprising SAP Security Branch officer, John Steyn, had taken it upon himself to train up 20 Himba tribesmen as Special Constables and to deploy them to counter SWAPO. Mounted in a Ribbok 4x4, the team would conduct operations to gather intelligence, identify spoor and track down SWAPO.

Dreyer was impressed with Steyn's work and incorporated the team into Koevoet's orbat. Based in Opuwo, he equipped the team with Casspirs and Buffel MPVs. This gave Z5S the essential mobility it required especially as it was becoming apparent that SWAPO's intention to establish a permanent presence in the area.

Similarly, to counter increasing SWAPO infiltration in the Kavango, in April 1981, Dreyer despatched Chris de Wit and his ZW call-sign to conduct screening operations there. The result being that Koevoet established an operations base at Rundu, out of which was deployed Z4C and Z4B. Tasked to counter SWAPO infiltration and insurgent activity in the Kavango and out east, along the cut line to the Caprivi, these teams each operated with four Casspirs and an early version of the Blesbok mine-protected logistics vehicle, which was utilised for the carriage of rations, ammunition, water

When one echelon was working, the other would be stood down giving the opportunity for much needed vehicle maintenance, weapon cleaning, stores checks and other unit admin. (Jim Hooper)

and other stores equipment. By now, Dreyer had split each of the call-signs into an A and B echelon. When the A echelon was deployed on operations, the B echelon would be in camp resting, training or conducting administrative tasks;

> Typically, two combat groups of four armoured personnel carriers and one supply vehicle each worked together, one group or team – the teams were interchangeable – stopping at a kraal, the second leapfrogging ahead to the next kraal, trackers debussing to question the PBs. Had they seen any SWAPO? When did they pass? How many, What weapons? Which direction were they moving?[3]

With Koevoet now operating out of bases in Ovambo, Kaokoland and the Kavango, the South Africans were now able to deploy a trained and aggressive COIN capability across the whole of northern Namibia. As it grew in experience, Dreyer and his leaders continued to develop Koevoet's ways of working such it was becoming a well-honed machine. Whilst continuous evolution was at the core of Koevoet's approach to COIN, patrolling, operations and pursuits would fall into a similar pattern. By mid-1981, this essentially took the form of:

- A team of 40 Special Constables deployed in four Casspirs with a logistics vehicle in support. Furthermore, a signals capability with which to call in additional Koevoet call-signs or SAAF aviation assets such as helicopter gunships or casevac
- The team work to acquire intelligence through investigative police work, liaison and engagement with the local population; routine and targeted questioning
- Upon intelligence received, deep patrolling of areas where last known sightings of insurgents occurred
- On identifying a suspected spoor, ready assessment of how old the spoor is – minutes, hours? – the number of insurgents and their relative fitness, weight of weapons and equipment carried
- On signalling the pursuit, the deployment of trackers on trackers would on foot with the Casspirs following behind in column of route or line abreast
- As and when required, rotation of the deployed trackers with those mounted in the Casspirs, this to maintain momentum – the trackers running light with just their small arms, R4 or R5 rifles, pistols; the weapon systems mounted on the Casspirs readied for immediate action
- When visual contact with the insurgents occurs, the deployed trackers and the Casspirs manoeuvre and vector onto the enemy; generating the maximum possible lethal force with which to win the firefight

Experienced senior NCOs – Koevoet presented opportunities for the Ovambos to earn promotion and pay. These experienced NCOs were invaluable to the South Africans. An Ovambo Warrant Officer would be appointed to command the Ovambo trackers in a call-sign. Each Casspir or 'car' team was commanded by a suitably experienced black or white operator and the team complement would usually include a sergeant. The remainder of the team being constables. (Jim Hooper)

- The combined mounted and deployed trackers conduct a final assault to neutralise the enemy
- Any wounded are treated, prisoners processed, dead accounted for, and the bodies prepared for transport to base for formal identification

This fast moving and adaptive approach sought to make the best use of the call-sign's available weapon systems – the light arms carried by the trackers and the 7.62mm and Browning .50-calibre combinations mounted on the Casspirs. It also looked to deliver a unity of effort with the trackers working in concert, rotating from their vehicles to the ground and vice versa, so long as their individual physical endurance allowed, and to maximise coordination with other assets such as other Koevoet call-signs and the SAAF gunships, should the need arise. The coordination of the above leading to a what could be called a 'COIN synchronisation.' The synergistic effect of drawing multiple assets to one kinetic point with which to neutralise the insurgents through the deployment of lethal force.

Koevoet was now presenting a unique set of COIN and direct combat skills. Its call-signs were able to manoeuvre by vehicle, conduct foot patrols, mount standing patrols and, in every instance, switch quick to pursuit, search and destroy. Its leaders, call-sign leaders, car commanders and trackers were becoming ever more experienced, and this led to a more formal organisational and command structure. There were opportunities for both black Special Constables and the white SAP officers to secure promotion and this was readily sought; bringing rank, enhanced status, privilege, better pay and service conditions to all.

Call-sign leaders had until 1981 always been white, but this was changing. Leadership positions was secured through experience, merit and operational prowess, not by rank. A Casspir commander might be a constable or a warrant officer, and it was not uncommon to see newly arrived and inexperienced white SAP officers 'commanded' by a black NCO. In practical terms, Koevoet assigned

The first mine-protected vehicles to serve with Koevoet were three Hippos. Also classified as an armoured personnel carrier, this type was specially designed to counter the threat of land mines deployed by SWAPO in northern Ovamboland in the early 1970s. Based on the chassis of the Bedford RL truck, it had a blast-proof hull and a troop compartment with seats facing inwards, and plate glass windows providing some visibility to passengers while still under protection. Each could carry 11 infantrymen in addition to the crew of two, and was equipped with interior water tanks, additional rifle racks and turrets for heavy weapons, primarily FN MAGs, Browning M1919s, and captured PKMs. Later on, at least one was equipped with a captured ZPU-2 14.5mm anti-aircraft gun and another with a French 20mm MG-151 cannon. (Artwork by David Bocquelet)

The Ribbok was another early mine-resistant vehicle of the SADF. Based on the Ford 4x4 Land Cruiser (or 'bakkie') chassis, it was developed in the early 1970s by the SAP as a five-seat vehicle affording a low-level of small arms- and mine-protection. However, it was to prove totally inadequate against anti-tank and reinforced mines frequently laid by the insurgents. With a road range of 1,000km it allowed the early Koevoet teams to conduct general policing and investigation work with some degree of protection. A total of 193 were built, of which 86 were for the SAP and 106 for use by government departments and private persons, like farmers and others living in or adjacent to the 'Operational Area'. (Artwork by David Bocquelet)

Based on the chassis of the Mercedes-Benz Unimog S truck, and developed in response to the increased use of mines by SWAPO, the Buffel was the second mass-produced, open-topped APC with a V-shaped hull to enter service with the SADF. Powered by the same Mercedes-Benz OM352, 6-cylinder, water-cooled diesel engine as the Unimog, it was designed for the difficult, off-road terrain of the African battlespace, and had high ground clearance. Koevoet deployed it for patrolling the Caprivi Strip and, because it provided protection not only against anti-tank mines, but also small arms fire and shrapnel, for COIN operations. (Artwork by David Bocquelet)

The standard armament of the Buffel included a single, pintle-mounted 7.62mm machine gun, located on the forward right-hand side of the passenger tub. Twin mountings with shields became more widespread during the mid-1980s. Custom tailored to provide mine-protection on roads or in areas where this threat was high, it proved its worth beyond any doubt. Buffels are known to have been hit by a total of 246 mines in southern Angola and northern South West Africa, and 19 out of 2,706 personnel carried by them were killed, and 453 injured. (Artwork by David Bocquelet)

The Casspir mine-protected vehicle was developed specifically with the SAP and CSIR in mind for COIN operations. Upon service entry in the early 1980s, its unique shape and profile became synonymous with Koevoet. The Casspir was powered by a 6-cylinder, turbo-charged 160hp engine, and was designed for the African battlespace: its 4x4 capability was exceptional, providing good off-road capability, mine-protection, field-repairability, and sufficient armour against small arms fire – all of which were of particular use in pursuit of insurgents. Originally, the Casspirs came without any armament as standard, but Koevoet quickly began arming them with single or twin Browning M1919 machine guns, as shown here. (Artwork by David Bocquelet)

In addition to their high mobility and reliability on all sorts of local terrain, Casspirs proved highly versatile due their other design features. One of these was the installation of a 200-litre water tank, highly appreciated by their crews and passengers during longer patrols. Another was the installation of at least two reserve wheels on every vehicle: often on either side of the central hull, in other cases high at the rear end of the superstructure, as shown here. In addition to Browning M1919 machine guns, at least 10 Casspirs were outfitted with 20mm cannons; a few section commanders replaced the single Browning with a twin-mount; while others mounted the Soviet-made 14.5mm KPV/KPVT heavy machine guns instead. (Artwork by David Bocquelet)

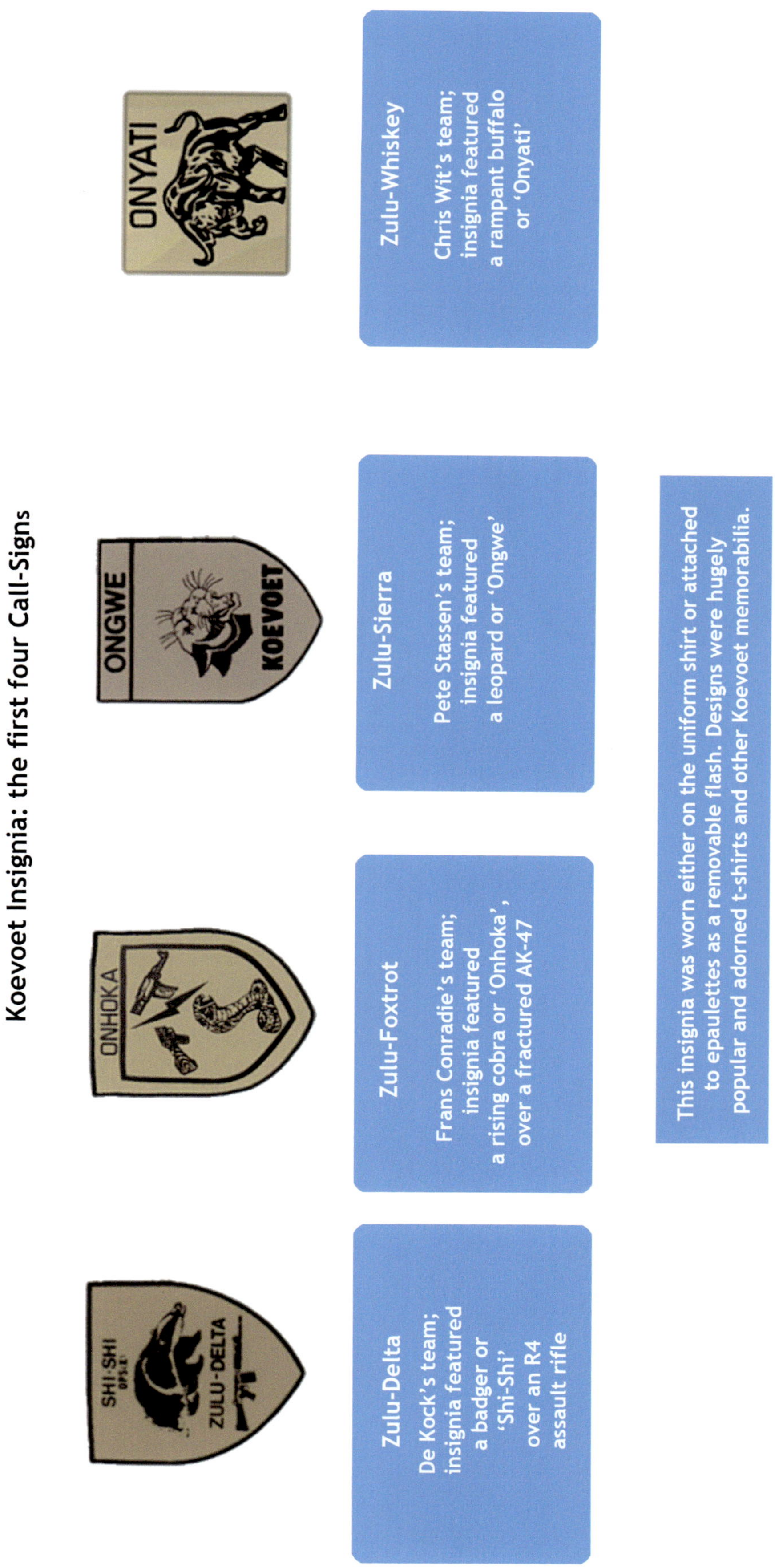

Koevoet Insignia: the first four Call-Signs

Zulu-Delta
De Kock's team; insignia featured a badger or 'Shi-Shi' over an R4 assault rifle

Zulu-Foxtrot
Frans Conradie's team; insignia featured a rising cobra or 'Onhoka', over a fractured AK-47

Zulu-Sierra
Pete Stassen's team; insignia featured a leopard or 'Ongwe'

Zulu-Whiskey
Chris Wit's team; insignia featured a rampant buffalo or 'Onyati'

This insignia was worn either on the uniform shirt or attached to epaulettes as a removable flash. Designs were hugely popular and adorned t-shirts and other Koevoet memorabilia.

The first four combat teams of the Koevoet, in order of their establishment. (Diagram by Author)

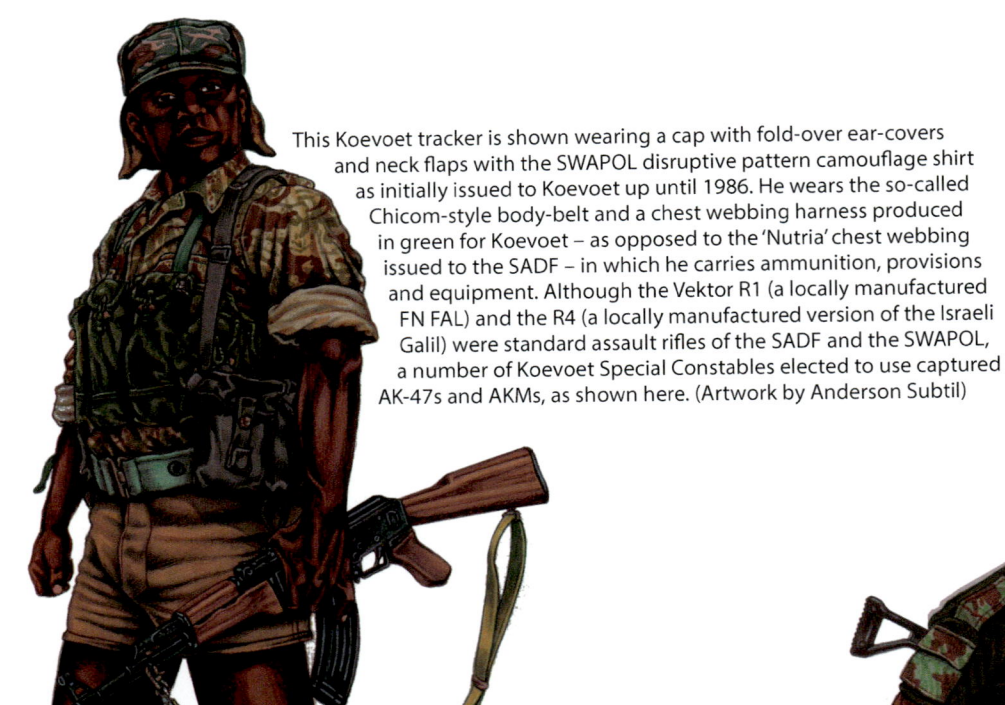

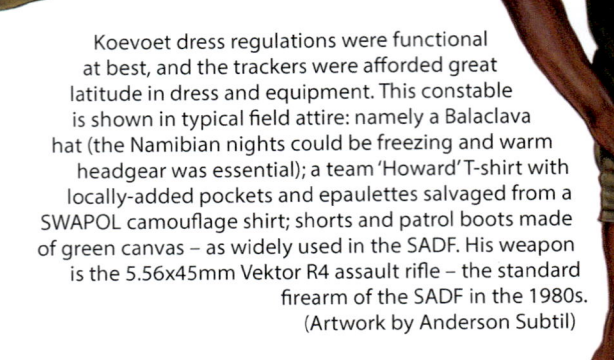

This Koevoet tracker is shown wearing a cap with fold-over ear-covers and neck flaps with the SWAPOL disruptive pattern camouflage shirt as initially issued to Koevoet up until 1986. He wears the so-called Chicom-style body-belt and a chest webbing harness produced in green for Koevoet – as opposed to the 'Nutria' chest webbing issued to the SADF – in which he carries ammunition, provisions and equipment. Although the Vektor R1 (a locally manufactured FN FAL) and the R4 (a locally manufactured version of the Israeli Galil) were standard assault rifles of the SADF and the SWAPOL, a number of Koevoet Special Constables elected to use captured AK-47s and AKMs, as shown here. (Artwork by Anderson Subtil)

Koevoet dress regulations were functional at best, and the trackers were afforded great latitude in dress and equipment. This constable is shown in typical field attire: namely a Balaclava hat (the Namibian nights could be freezing and warm headgear was essential); a team 'Howard' T-shirt with locally-added pockets and epaulettes salvaged from a SWAPOL camouflage shirt; shorts and patrol boots made of green canvas – as widely used in the SADF. His weapon is the 5.56x45mm Vektor R4 assault rifle – the standard firearm of the SADF in the 1980s. (Artwork by Anderson Subtil)

In 1986, Dreyer instructed Koevoet to adopt an olive green uniform similar in pattern to the SADF-issue Nutria clothing. With wear and laundering, this olive green faded quickly to a grey-green colour. As well as wearing pants and a cap in this pattern, this combatant is shown wearing a camouflage blouse – probably captured from the Angolans – and a holster for his, presumably also captured, Soviet-made Makorov T-30 pistol. (Artwork by Anderson Subtil)

The Aérospatiale SE.316B Alouette III was a single-engine, light utility helicopter developed by French aircraft company Sud Aviation in the early 1960s. It was the SAAF's standard light helicopter, and more than 120 airframes were procured. In support of Koevoet, it performed several roles including command, liaison, spotting, casualty evacuation and gunship support. Shown here is the typical 'G-Car': the sub-variant armed with two side-mounted 0.30 Brownings (re-bored to 7.62mm; and sometimes replaced by a single FN MAG 7.62mm machine gun), which usually also carried a 'stick' of four to five troops. (Artwork by Luca Canossa)

Another sub-variant of the SAAF Alouette IIIs that saw involvement in operations in support of Koevoet was the 'K-Car': this was equipped for command and fire-support roles, including a single MG.151 20mm autocannon installed in the rear cabin, which fired through the port door opening and proved devastatingly effective. The Koevoet/SAAF partnership was to prove highly effective and frequent pursuits were successfully concluded as a result of joint work with the Alouette crews. (Artwork by Luca Canossa)

The Sud Aviation (later Aérospatiale) SA.330 Puma was the SAAF's principal medium-lift helicopter, used for troop transport, assault, logistics, and casualty evacuation. It was frequently deployed in support of Koevoet operations, where the teams referred to the Pumas as 'giants'. Its excellent four-blade rotor, powered by twin engines, gave it high speed and significant agility, and many an injured tracker owned his life to the fearless crews ready to conduct casualty evacuation under fire. (Artwork by Tom Cooper)

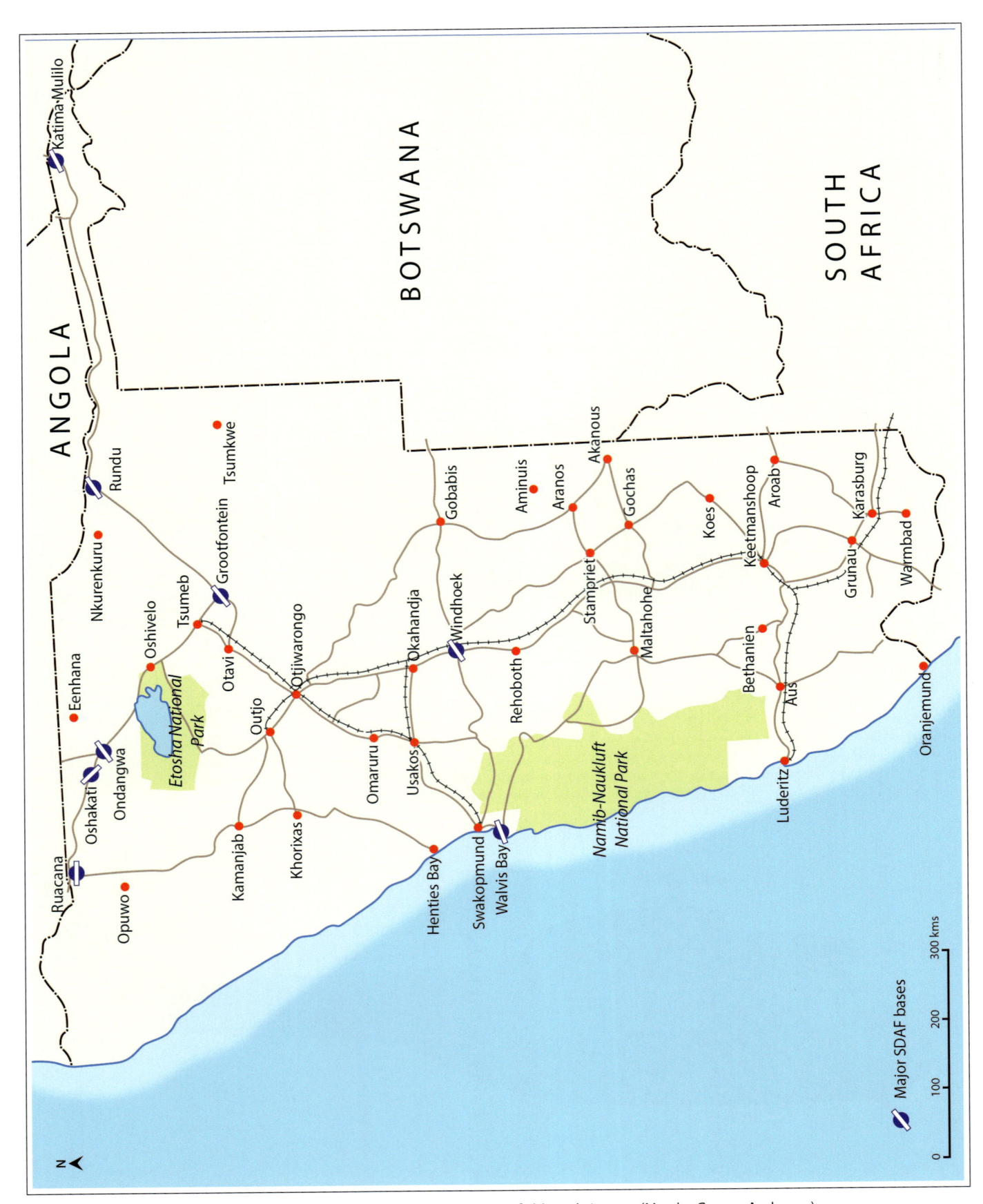

A map of South West Africa during the 1980s showing the most important airfields and airports. (Map by George Anderson)

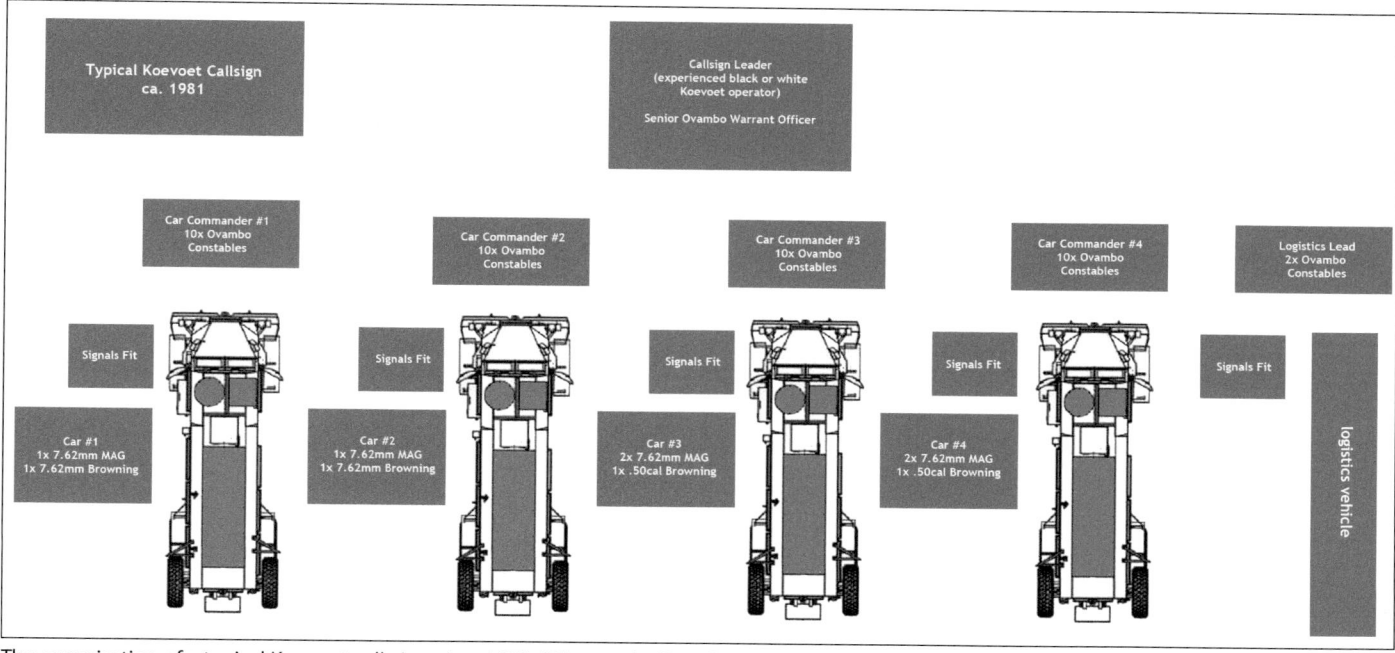

The organisation of a typical Koevoet call-sign circa 1981. (Diagram by Tom Cooper)

field leadership to whoever first identified a spoor. They would then lead the advance to contact and command the subsequent and ensuing action.

Approximately 40 Ovambo constables and five white SAP officers would constitute the call-sign. Car commanders night be Ovambos or white, dependent upon experience and merit. The call-sign leader would be a white SAP officer working closely with his senior Ovambo warrant officer who, in turn, would be responsible for the operational effectiveness of the Ovambos, their administration and welfare. The relationship between the call-sign leader and the senior warrant officer was clearly critical; 'I was very fortunate to have an extremely capable Warrant Officer in Jesaya Mulayi, a Kwanyama from Angola, as my black team leader. The Ovambo team members had the utmost respect for him, with the result that we never had any petty nonsense in the team.'[4]

Oshakati continued to develop as Dreyer's headquarters with the ongoing addition of stores compounds, holding cells for captured insurgents, armoury and vehicle workshops. The need to maintain vehicles was a continuing pressure for Koevoet. Dreyer could ill afford to have Casspirs and other support vehicles 'off-road.' Accordingly, Koevoet's blue-overalled mechanics – or 'Blue Bells' as they became known – worked tirelessly to keep the vehicles operational. Originally the mechanics were drawn from the SAP on three-month rotations, but eventually the billets were occupied by SWAPOL mechanics. Smashed suspensions and damaged drive trains were a common occurrence when traversing the thick bush or

Call-sign members replace a Casspir suspension assembly in the field. If the damage was particularly severe, mechanics would be flown out from Oshakati. (Jim Hooper)

when 'bundu bashing.' Fortunately, the Casspir had been designed so that suspension springs and drive train could be replaced with comparative ease. If a mine-strike or other occurrence had rendered the vehicle immobile, then the mechanics would be flown out to the location to effect field repairs. Failing such, the vehicle would be recovered to the base workshop by a heavy lift Mercedes platform and in later years, a Wolf Turbo recovery vehicle. On other occasions the SADF would be requested to assist with its heavy lift platforms.

Each call-sign was expected to keep its Casspir serviceable and it would be seen as a last resort if a team had to have its vehicle recovered or left 'Vehicle Off Road' (VOR) in the workshops;

Real vehicle maintenance was very simply taught to the newest member of every team: "Go to the 'Blue Bells' and fix this car. Don't come back until it is fixed." No manuals, no instruction or drawings and only some very pedantic short term South Africa based mechanics on hand from the mechanical school in Benoni mostly, whom were much more insistent on following the teatime and lunch roster rather than fixing abused iron cars. Sink or swim was a very effective mechanical training tool. Do not for one moment imagine if you screwed up, that "I didn't know" would be an acceptable defense. In fact, it would be seen as deliberately sabotaging the team's success rate and serious hell would find its way to you soon, from your own team mates!![5]

With Koevoet's penchant for innovation, the vehicles were constantly improved and upgraded upon. Working together, the Koevoet mechanics and call-sign leaders 'added protection plates over all the hydraulic pipes, differentials and transfer boxes, got rid of the metal mudguards and replaced them with conveyer belting (less shrapnel from landmines), added metal grilles with which to protect the radiators.'[6] With these additions, the Koevoet Casspirs or 'cars', as they were commonly called, were to become robust and agile manoeuvre platforms which were to add much to Koevoet's tactical signature.

The Evolution of Koevoet's Dress and Insignia

Alongside the development of Koevoet's headquarter facilities, its doctrine, operational tactics and systems came uniformity of dress. At the beginning, Dreyer's men were attired in whatever could be begged, borrowed or stolen. This would see trackers attired in a mix of SADF 'browns', SAP camouflage, civilian boiler suits and, in some instances, combat clothing of Rhodesian origin. This motley assortment was occasionally supplemented with captured uniforms which, invariably, originated from Warsaw Pact stocks. Eventually Koevoet was scaled in the camouflage uniform used by the SWAPOL. This was a disruptive pattern developed in South Africa of bush brown and green upon a sand base. The uniform was made out of a heavy cotton fabric and available as a series of clothing items – shorts, long trousers, shirts, field jackets and a peaked cap with a sunscreen flap for the neck (which was usually cut off).

Utility and ease of wear was critical to Koevoet and there was great latitude in how the white SAP officers and the black Special Constables were dressed and equipped. Woollen balaclavas were common and for the freezing Ovambo nights, jumpers of SADF and SAP origin were popular. Footwear was again subject to personal preference, but in the early days, leather SAP boots were issued which were to be later superseded by green and khaki Israeli 'Scout' boots.

A key item of Koevoet dress was the green SAP 'Howard' T-shirt. These were worn both as an undergarment and as a standalone camouflage layer during hot weather. Teams would frequently produce their own T-shirts which would be adorned with their respective call-sign insignia or chosen character. All of this helped to build the desired and idealised identity Dreyer and his leaders

Koevoet recruits parade in the early issue SWAPOL camouflage. This was superseded in 1986 by an olive green uniform, as seen on the white officer, which was designed to differentiate Koevoet from the SAP STF who continued to wear camouflage. (Jim Hooper)

Members of call-sign Zulu Alpha conduct a map appreciation. Visible is the emblazoned T-shirt with the team logo on the left breast, a frightened insurgent jumping over a cobra, and the team initials on the right shoulder. These T-shirts were locally produced and very popular. They continue to be reproduced today. (Jim Hooper)

The scorpion, rampant, is the centrepiece of the Zulu 4 Sierra team insignia, adorning a locally manufactured T-shirt. These insignias were very popular, and the trackers would be especially proud of their team 'brand.' (Authors Collection)

The first issue and early Koevoet tupperware flash (called 'tupperware' because they were printed on a cheap rubberised plastic) that was worn by all ranks on both shoulders. Affixed to the epaulette it features the baton of South Africa – blue, white, orange – adorned with the title 'Koevoet' above the SWAPOL star. Interestingly this example is from a batch where the baton colours were incorrectly printed as blue, white and red as opposed to the required red. (Authors collection)

wanted Koevoet to become; a relatively small but cohesive and effective COIN capability. One that was aggressive and fearless in its pursuit of insurgents. The use of insignia to promote this unit identity was much encouraged; 'Each team had its own T-shirt and totem – an elephant, lion, badger or scorpion, a lynx, snake crocodile or other creature considered dangerous or disagreeable. The T-shirts invariably showed an AK-47 broken in half.[7]

Reproduced on beer mugs, plaques and ash trays, these call-sign insignias helped foster team rivalries and to build a collective sense of mission purpose. This was reflected in Koevoet's official heraldry which featured the South West African coat of arms, set within the SAP star and sat below a 'balkie' or bar with the title, 'Koevoet.' Fashioned as cloth shields, these emblazonments were worn as shoulder flashes and over time, were produced in the rubberised 'tupperware' format common to the SADF. Whilst Koevoet, at the height of its existence, only numbered 42 call-signs, there were many variants of these differing shoulder flashes, as local fashions changed, and team leaders came and went.

Throughout 1981, Koevoet worked to consolidate its expansion and to dominate its new and enlarged area of operations. Unlike the SADF that conducted its COIN and warfighting operations through offensive externals such as Op Sceptic and Op Protea, Koevoet's actions were less set-piece. The ongoing investigative police work, the tracking of spoor, the advance to contact and the culminating action, continued day in, day out with Koevoet achieving considerable success;

In 1979, they killed 64 insurgents and captured/arrested 65 in 40 contacts. Own casualties were three dead and two wounded.

In 1980, they killed 105 and captured 27 in 88 contacts, suffering own casualties of two dead and eight wounded.

In 1981, they killed 434 and captured 79 in 256 contacts. Their own casualties were four dead and 64 wounded.[8]

There was no doubting that the insurgents were proving to be a formidable and, at times, elusive enemy. SWAPO's own intelligence capabilities were thought to be excellent, aided and abetted by an extensive network of spies and informers. Indeed, arrest operations would have to be carefully planned so as to avoid the risk of tip off

The call-sign tupperware flash for team Zulu 1 Juliet which operated out of Ongwediva (Zulu 1). The flash features the wildcat Caracal which is native to Namibia. (Authors collection)

and compromise. Koevoet's leadership were convinced that some of the indigenous SWAPOL officers were also sympathetic to SWAPO and so were alerting SWAPO to Koevoet intentions. Clearly SWAPO was at an advantage. Its fighters originated from the local population, could speak the tribal languages and so could melt seamlessly into the community. Its leadership was receiving political, civil society and military training in China and North Korea, and its insurgent, warfighting prowess was increasing. The size of the insurgent groups infiltrating into Namibia was also increasing as was their boldness and sophistication. The groups usually included a political commissar who would work to disseminate political and Marxist doctrine alongside the fighters. This to get the local population onside and to create a micro-climate that presented the South African occupation as illegal, corrupted and degraded; an occupation with no political legitimacy and which was inherently unstable, leading to a fragility that could easily be challenged by SWAPO. With cultural support and a local population that was supportive of the liberation struggle, the South Africans would have to use all their resources to counter SWAPO, who saw themselves as facing

> ... a bewildering variety of military, paramilitary and police units deployed in Namibia in defence of South Africa's illegal occupation ... Some of the forces ... operate in a deliberately low-profile, even clandestine manner ... The personnel ... includes full-timers and part-timers; professionals, volunteers and conscripts; forces permanently based in Namibia, and forces based in South Africa but doing tours of duty in, or seconded to Namibia.[9]

SWAPO also found itself responding to the South Africans' continued efforts to 'Nambianise' the war, citing that Pretoria had; 'introduced 'ethnic units' whereby Namibians have been recruited and trained to fight against SWAPO.'[10]

Yet for Dreyer in 1981, it was a lack of cooperation between Koevoet and the SADF that was exasperating his efforts to tackle the insurgency; 'Koevoet teams lacked logistical support and so relied on the army for fuel, some repairs and medical support. This led to many conflicts between the two commanders, Brigadier Hans Dreyer (Koevoet – SAP) and Brigadier 'Witkop' Badenhorst (Sector 10 – SADF). On one occasion Badenhorst threatened to charge me if I supported Koevoet logistically again. I ignored the threat for there was a goal to achieve.'[11] Matters were not to improve until 1982 when Badenhorst was promoted and returned to the 'States', that is – South Africa. In the meantime, Dreyer worked to maintain the initiative through maximising the use of 'turned fighters' and the development of an informer network which was aimed at securing ready Human Intelligence (HUMINT) to counter the work of SWAPO's political commissars and the insurgent threat.

The shock of capture. Whilst this image was taken in 1986, it illustrates members of call-sign Zulu Hotel readying SWAPO insurgent Martin Haungula for despatch to the rear. An Ovambo and fluent in Afrikaans, Huangula had been recruited by SWAPO 10 years previously. Promised access to education and money, he had received little training and was on his third incursion into Namibia. (Jim Hooper)

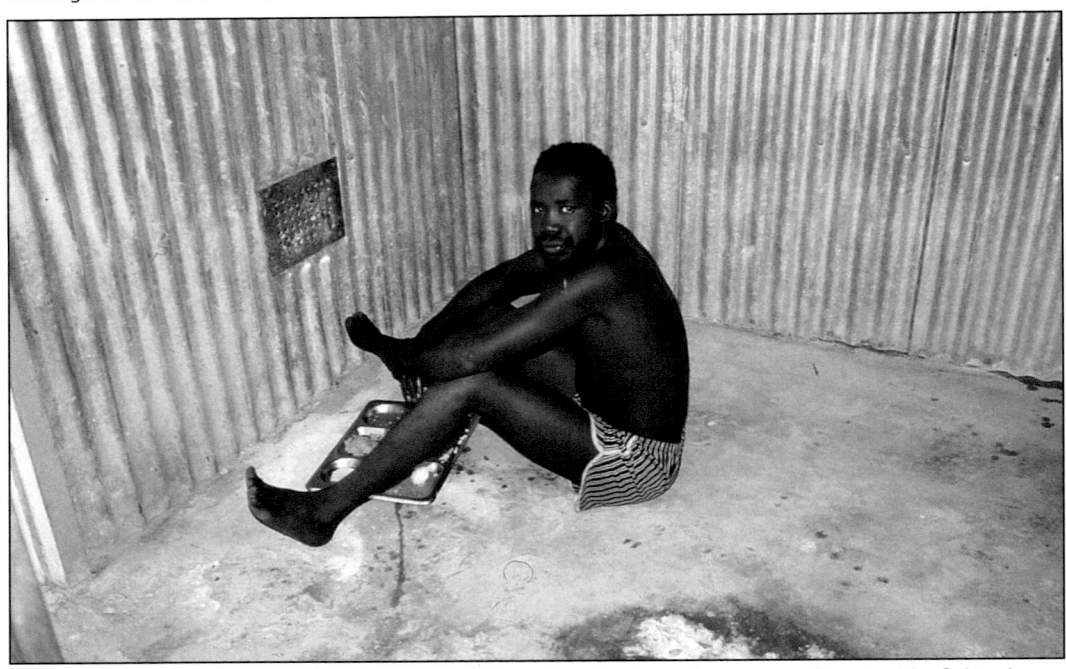

The dislocation of expectation. Placed into the holding cells at Eenhana, the process of 'turning' the fighter has begun. (Jim Hooper)

The Turning of Former Fighters

The turning of former insurgents, whether SWAPO activists or PLAN fighters was to prove especially important for Koevoet;

> ... later we caught John Sam. He joined us and became a loyal and fearless fighter. He was also an important source of information. He knew a lot and was trained in the USSR and Libya. He had been

a senior PLAN commander and knew intimately the operational thought patterns and modus operandi of SWAPO. We fetched his wife and children and gave him a house at Rundu.[12]

At one point it was thought that at least half of the Koevoet black constables were former fighters, though there is some suggestion that South Africa 'exaggerated the 'turned' factor to mask Koevoet's dependence on Angolans.'[13]

For those fighters captured by the Koevoet call-signs, surrendering and 'turning' to the other side meant living another day. Invariably the fighter would be assigned to the call-sign that had captured him and required to provide local intelligence and insight. Often the turned fighter would be required to take on the role of 'interrogator' – questioning his former comrades as to PLAN and SWAPO intentions. Word would then get back to the fighter's insurgent and village that yet another had been 'turned' to join Koevoet. The chance of any previously 'turned' fighter being rehabilitated back into SWAPO were nil. SWAPO itself was known to be ruthless in its persecution of dissenters or those that failed to support the liberation struggle. Indeed, any member of SWAPO suspected of links to the apartheid regime or of 'anti-revolutionary' activities might find themselves detained in a SWAPO holding facility; 'Long-time insurgents suspected of being spies were subjected to prolonged nights of torture, during which they made false confessions. None were ever brought to trial or put through any legal process.'[14] Many were simply murdered.

Turning was one of the keys to Koevoet's success. Any turned fighter would be watched closely until they had proved their worth and utility to the call-signs, often operating unarmed until their commitment to the unit had been evidenced. These turned fighters 'had been part of the SWAPO insurgency force, or they were locals who chose to defect, generally because the SADF co-erced them. As a result, they were fighting their former comrades or fellow Namibians.'[15]

Koevoet's use of Informers

Koevoet made extensive use of informers and saw their use as both necessary and legitimate. Some simply provided single event or occasional or 'tip offs' to the call-signs, others yielded more substantial and regular information, over a longer time frame, often in concert with a Koevoet handler who would invariably 'run' them and pay for the intelligence secured.

These informers were drawn from a wide circle. Some were members of the local population living in the various rural kraals that dotted Ovamboland, others were civic officials who were able to move around the operational area in the course of their official duties. A number were members of SWAPO who were, quite simply, spying for the South Africans – 'insiders' who took it upon themselves to betray SWAPO. Clearly high-risk behaviour that would result in certain death should they be discovered.

The principal use of informers in a COIN scenario is to secure information and intelligence that the state agency is not, ordinarily, able to access. In addition, informers can be used to destabilise insurgent movements by spreading distrust, confusion or fear. This can weaken a movement as it conducts internal witch-hunts in pursuit of possible informers or spies, whilst also posing a legacy challenge that may persist once the conflict has ended; this compounding a community's potential to rehabilitate after armed confrontation. Suspicion as to who was an informer or 'grass' may persist for decades. Today, the US government is particularly challenged as it seeks to provide safe harbour to those Afghan informers who provided intelligence on the Taliban and Al-Qaeda to the CIA, the Taliban government making no secret of its intention to seek out and punish those who worked for NATO.

Koevoet's use of informers was particularly effective;

We had many informers all over our area of operation. These people would supply us with information of what was happening in their area. Many a time they were people who had had a bad experience with SWAPO, or sometimes they were members of SWAPO who had become disillusioned by what it was doing: intimidation, kidnappings and landmines hurt the local population, their people.[16]

Funds were available to pay informers and the quality of information they yielded appeared to be good. Throughout the insurgency, informers provided Dreyer and his men with details of individual fighters, insurgent movements, weapon types, the movement of ordnance, planned and anticipated operations. A small number of especially 'loyal' informers were deployed to sabotage planned SWAPO operations. To open up hidden weapon caches to the elements or to render ordnance types unusable.

Koevoet trackers question a local hunter. Through investigative policing, the use of informers and the interrogation of captured insurgents, the teams were able to build a HUMINT picture with which to plan operations though ever agile, Koevoet would often react in real-time to insurgent activity. (Jim Hooper)

The South Africans were to use informers and spies to great effect. Indeed, at one point it was reported that a network of at least 100 spies had been detected in SWAPO offices in Zambia and Angola. Four of whom were members of SWAPO's central policy making committee. Both SWAPO and PLAN were infiltrated by the South Africans who used direct threats to force persons of interest to inform and spy on their behalf. Not unlike the fighters turned by Koevoet call-signs, many informers had little choice, despite the possible risk of being identified and exposed as betrayers. For these individuals, they were to live a challenged life – under threat from the South Africans charging them to inform, and at risk of exposure to SWAPO who saw themselves as the ascendent power that would, one day, punish treason and betrayal in order to affirm its newly won legitimacy.

This threat of condemnation and death was heightened by SWAPO's political commissars who portrayed informers as 'folk devils' who purposefully spread disunity and disruption. This notion of 'devils', in turn further legitimising SWAPO's right to define and punish. The holding of impromptu trials for suspected informers was a common SWAPO tactic with summary execution often an outcome. This, sometimes, including the supposed informer's whole family, who would also be executed without trial or reason.

6
1982 – Operation Yahoo: Collaboration with the SADF

In March 1982, SWAPO attempted a large-scale infiltration into Namibia. The incursion saw approximately 300 insurgents in various fighting groups deployed to infiltrate below what was called the 'Red Line', a cleared gap some 200 metres wide which divided the white farming areas from the northern tribal lands. Bisecting both Ovamboland and the Kavango, this line was sensitive to the South Africans. The presence of any SWAPO insurgents or PLAN fighters south of the line would be cause for real concern, suggesting an insurgent threat to Grootfontein and the towns to the south; a geography that was colloquially referred to as the 'death triangle.' This being the districts of Tsumeb, Otavi and Grootfontein, which lay within the SADF's Sector 30 area of operations.

Dreyer initially tasked call-sign Zulu Lima to track this infiltration, but the spoor was washed out by the torrential rains of the rainy season that had just commenced. Another incursion was identified towards the end of the month but, again, the spoor was lost to the rains. It was clear to the South African's that this year's 'Summer Games' were to be larger than before and that a major SWAPO action was in the offing. Hence, the SADF placed its units on standby to react and a tactical headquarters, reporting to the SWATF command, was established at Tsumeb. The mechanised infantry battalion, 61 Mech, was ordered to move its Ratel-mounted fighting units to the north from southern Ovamboland and to take up positions in and around in Tsumeb. In all, some 3,000 SADF personnel were mobilised, and the SAAF were tasked to assist, with helicopters and fixed wing assets placed on standby.

Given the anticipated scale of the SWAPO incursion, the SADF commander, Commandant Serfontein, formally requested Koevoet's assistance as part of the response manoeuvre which had been titled Operation Yahoo. Dreyer complied and a number of call-signs were placed under temporary army command with Koevoet officers embedded into the tactical headquarters. The SADF offered full echelon support to the Koevoet teams including accommodation, rations, fuel and other stores.

The Koevoet teams were immediately tasked to commence patrolling so as to identify any possible infiltrations. Yet, initially, leads were difficult to come by and there were no positive sightings. However, on 8 April, a kraal head reported that some 90 insurgents had passed through his settlement and were seen to be heading to the south. This was just adjacent to the Angolan border by what was known as 'Beacon 32.' This being one of a series of 47 numbered beacons that run along the border from east to west; number one being in the west, number 47 being the furthest beacon in the east. These cement beacons were about a metre high and a metre square at the base tapering up to a squared-off top. Used as readily identifiable reference points, one side was inscribed 'SWA' and on the other 'Angola.'

Very quickly, four Koevoet call-signs – Zulu Golf, Zulu Papa, Zulu Tango and Zulu Yankee – were assembled to effect pursuit. The evident spoor was readily identified – 90 insurgents on the move leave a significant spoor and are easily tracked – and led the teams to a number of recently prepared defensive positions. Upon examination, these positions were found to be abandoned and so the call-signs continued their pursuit.

Further defensive positions were found and then, chancing upon a kraal, confirmation was secured that approximately 100–120 insurgents had passed through an hour previously. To assist identification and to add gunship support, the Koevoet call-signs called in SAAF support in the form of two Alouette III helicopters and a fixed wing spotter plane flown by a reservist. Circling ahead, the pilot of the spotter aircraft announced some technical malfunction and to the horror of the observing call-signs, promptly crashed in a ball of flame. Both the pilot and the accompanying Koevoet spotter were killed. This galvanised the shocked call-signs into action who, in response, moved into a four-column order of march. Moving forward they continued their pursuit until they were hit by a deadly V-shaped ambush.

The action was sudden and brutal with the insurgent killing group concentrating their fire on the lead Casspirs. One immediately had its left tyre blown out by a hastily laid POM-Z anti-personnel mine and another was hit by an RPG-7 grenade, which killed three trackers and wounded the white car commander. Five out of the 16 Casspirs were hit by RPGs and HEAT STRIM rifle grenades. The firefight was intense and chaotic, yet Koevoet's proven tactics enabled the teams to conduct anti-ambush drills and to fight through the V-shaped killing zone. The resultant action saw 10 insurgents killed and the call-signs

> … recovered large quantities of war material in the area which indicated the infiltrating groups were heavily armed. Amongst the stuff captured was a PKM machine gun, two SKS carbines, seven AK-47s, 21 anti-personnel mines, 20 anti-tank rifle grenades, five 60mm mortar bombs, seven POM-Z anti-personnel mines,

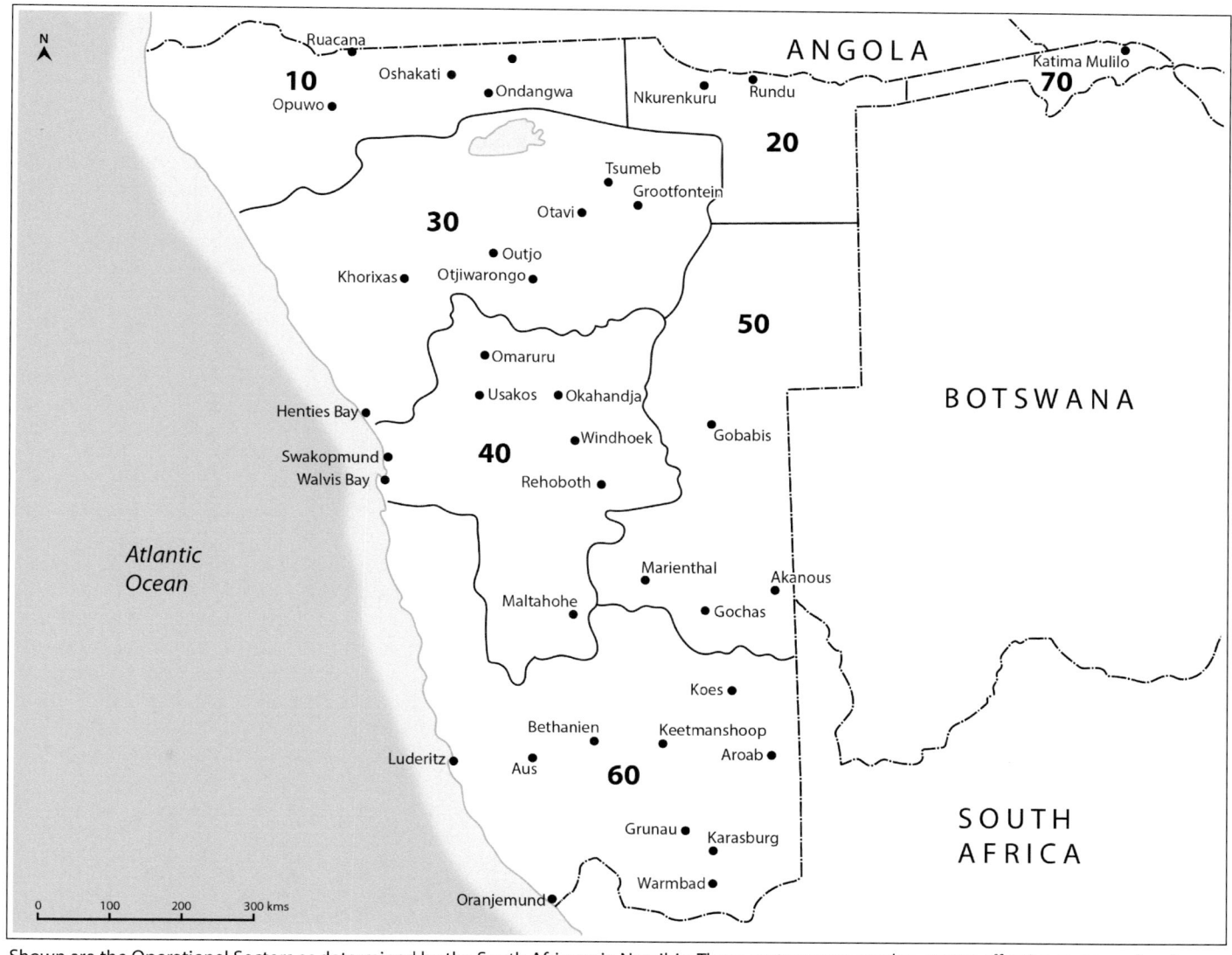

Shown are the Operational Sectors as determined by the South Africans in Namibia. These sectors were used to ensure effective command and control. Sectors 10, 20 and 70 were the 'frontline' sectors. Sector 30 was an intermediate buffer sector hosting the so-called 'triangle of death', whereas 40, 50 and 60 were more administrative sectors. Operation Yahoo saw SWAPO penetrate deep into Sector 30, much to the consternation of the South Africans. (Map by George Anderson)

seven RPG missiles, groundsheets, medical kits, ammunition and a great variety of other kit.[1]

This incident was just one of many as Koevoet worked to support Operation Yahoo. On 9 April, call-sign Zulu Echo picked up the spoor of 31 insurgents who had crossed the cutline by beacon five and who were heading south towards the Red Line. Three other call-signs joined Zulu Echo and on the morning of the 10 April, all teams mounted a pursuit. The spoor was tracked and an advance to contact occurred. The call-signs prosecuted the firefight killing five insurgents and taking one prisoner. Subsequent interrogation revealed that these insurgents were PLAN fighters from a 'Volcano' special unit, numbering 51 insurgents, with orders to kill white farmers, sabotage railway lines and destroy railway infrastructure.

The 'summer games' continued with SWAPO mounting further infiltrations. The tempo of operations intensified with the South Africans taking incurring losses. On 15 April, a 61 Mech armoured patrol was ambushed on the Red Line. As it approached a suspected insurgent crossing point, a Ratel IFV crew, accompanied by Bushmen trackers, noted what looked to be SWAPO propaganda leaflets scattered across the ground. Closer inspection revealed an evident spoor and signs of defensive positions. As the patrol commander ordered his Ratels to commence a search procedure, the patrol was ambushed and hit by RPG-7 rockets and HEAT STRIM rifle grenades. Ten of the 61 Mech soldiers were killed. As SAAF Puma helicopters moved into to recover the dead, they were forced to evade an SA-7 surface to air missile fired from the ground. The subsequent follow-up operation found that the Ratel patrol had fallen victim to a well-planned ambush. It had been laid out in a horseshoe fashion and featured well prepared emplacements from which the insurgents were able to discharge their weapons.

Koevoet continued to track the infiltrations daily, through April and into early May, tracing multiple spoors and conducting numerous follow-up actions, some of which were complex as the PLAN fighters kidnapped local civilians and pressed them into service. These were challenging times as the South Africans sought to counter the largest PLAN offensive to date and one that demonstrated PLAN's increasing use of elite units.

The PLAN 'Volcano' or 'Typhoon' units were a supposed elite who had received rigorous training in China and North Korea. Numbering some 400 fighters, these units were tasked for deep infiltration, sabotage and assassination, the laying of mines and conducting ambushes – otherwise known as 'Chicom Tactics' or Chinese Communist Tactics. Their principal aim was to strike deep

The SADF and Koevoet frequently worked together. Many of the young National Service 'troepies' were in awe of Koevoet. Here an SADF army engineer examines an anti-tank mine recovered during a joint operation. (Jim Hooper)

Yahoo allowed Dreyer to demonstrate the effectiveness of his COIN capability but it also highlighted weaknesses. Very simply, there were times when Koevoet was overwhelmed and so there was a need to expand the unit, modernise its vehicle fleet and upgrade its weaponry. More trained Koevoet assets were required if future 'summer games' were to be effectively countered.

But what Operation Yahoo did demonstrate was the potential for successful Koevoet/SADF collaboration. In October 1982, Koevoet operated for the first time in Angola. In support of the SADF it worked to dominate ground after the capture of Xangongo and Ondijiva from FAPLA. Intelligence suggested that there were sizable PLAN into Namibia and to hit the white farming areas. This to create fear, insecurity and instability, such that the farmers would abandon their holdings, affording SWAPO the opportunity to further maximise the fragility of the South African occupation.

These PLAN elite units were commanded by Danger Ashpala who was to eventually, after the war, secure a senior command position in the Namibian Defence Force. He was supported by an articulate and persuasive second-in-command, a political commissar named Kapoko. Well-motivated and well trained, Ashpala structured the Volcano and Typhoon units into platoons which each comprised approximately 35–40 fighters. Operating out of Lubango, these were capable adversaries who, at this time, did not fear Koevoet and were ready to take the fight to the South Africans.

Hence the 'summer games' continued with the PLAN fighters making best use of the lush vegetation for concealment and evading Koevoet by traversing the rocky terrain, south of the Red Line. Working through its informer network and with the real-time intelligence provided by the local population, Dreyer's leaders were able to note where and when the PLAN fighters had passed by. Over the years, the South Africans had built up a good intelligence infrastructure in the area. Linked to the existing good quality communications network, sightings could be advised by telephone. Add to this, the ease with which the Koevoet call-signs could move along the cleared cutlines, along with the presence of a tarred road network, PLAN were clearly at a distinct disadvantage. This even more so, given there were plenty of airstrips and airfields from which the SAAF helicopters could operate in support of Koevoet.

Eventually, the SADF began to assess that the tide was turning for the '1981 summer games'; 'the spoor of small groups marching north above the Red Line showed that at least some had had had enough and had either deserted or were 'going home' to Angola. There were numerous follow-ups. Koevoet groups aided by helicopter gunships relentlessly pursued and killed many of the withdrawing enemy.'[2]

Koevoet operated in support of Operation Yahoo till the end of May. It had been the biggest PLAN incursion of the Liberation War to date and one that had shocked the South Africans. For Koevoet, groups located to the north of these towns and so four Koevoet call-signs moved to Ondijiva from where they patrolled out to the west and east, accompanied by Parabats in Buffel MPVs; 'At a point west of Komatu about 30 kilometres north of the cutline, they picked up spoor of eight insurgents. They pursued them a long way and finally made contact. They shot seven of the eight. The group was heavily armed with AKs, SKSs, RGP-7s and high explosive anti-tank grenades.'[3]

Sensing that the 'summer games' were to become an annual offensive, Dreyer moved to establish a permanent Koevoet base in Tsumeb. The facility was sited at Mannheim Farm which was purchased in early 1983 exclusively for Koevoet's use. With the addition of offices, accommodation blocks and store sheds, the farm very quickly became an operational concern which, like the Koevoet base in Oshakati, was also to boast facilities for the training of Koevoet trackers in skills for life. This initiative was to see Dreyer work with University of Pretoria to design and develop a substantial agricultural enterprise through which his trackers, including turned fighters, could acquire food production and small scale enterprise skills. This programme was an immediate success and would be expanded further with the acquisition of Scott Farm, just to the north of Mannheim. Irrigation systems were laid, and the farms became home to livestock herds which sustained trackers, many of whom lived on the Tsumeb base with their families. The methodologies utilised on the 'Koevoet estate' were far in advance of those, ordinarily, used by the white farmers in the region and over time, this was to see a change in local attitudes to farming best practice – the laying of irrigation networks, the use of fertilisers and good animal husbandry.

In order to resource Koevoet's existing orbat and the new capability to be deployed to Tsumeb, along with the need to address the challenge of the 'summer games', Dreyer had to address Koevoet's manning liability and this meant the recruitment of additional white officers from the SAP and the SWAPOL, and the recruitment of more trackers. As Koevoet looked into and black Special Constables. In 1983, Koevoet was to expand and significantly so.

7
1983 – Koevoet Consolidates

The geographic expansion of Koevoet led to

> … an unprecedented recruitment drive in 1983, which resulted in a massive influx of hopefuls as the unit became better known. It also, unfortunately, resulted in a lot of chaff applying for all manner of reasons; however they were whittled down to the acceptable recruits. What the selection process missed was sorted out over time by a baptism of fire and gradual weeding out.[1]

The recruitment and training of recruits – both black and white – was now becoming refined, a process that had been developed during Koevoet's early years and which was continuously reviewed and improved upon, with the incorporation of learning from the field continuous and ongoing.

A critical consideration for Dreyer, as Koevoet looked to consolidate, was the quality of the men that applied to join its ranks;

> I must mention I am of the opinion that all people have the same capacity for learning. If a child exposed to modern amenities, toys and equipment goes to school, he would be literate within a few short years. A child devoid of these modern privileges will learn at the same rate, but his skills would be practical and his knowledge will reflect his natural surroundings. Take both to adulthood, one will be a matriculant on his way to become a Cop, the other an Ovambo with astonishing tracking and bush skills. Find a way to pair the two up, give them a worthy adversary, a very, very short command chain with a brilliant tactician in charge and you get Koevoet! Simple really!![2]

Koevoet recruited its white officers from the SAP and the SWAPOL. All applicants seeking to transfer to Koevoet were required to attend the SAP COIN Training course which had been significantly developed and improved upon since the SAP's early efforts in the late 1960s:

> SAP COIN training was very well structured (6 Weeks) with formal lectures, tactics and procedures. Very similar in structure to any normal infantry (British/Rhodesian) COIN training curriculum. The focus was on section (10 men) and platoon sized tactics. A little known fact was that South African Policemen went to war for more than a century as policemen! Border COIN duty was a reality and way of life for SAP members for almost two decades prior to the formation of Koevoet, including serving as BSAP members in PATU units in Rhodesia until the late seventies. Additional bush pay was of course money for jam as well as a break from much more mundane police bureaucracy for three months every year.
>
> About 10% of SAP Coin course graduates remained behind to attend a mortar course (One additional week) using 60mm Hotchkiss-Brandt mortars. This did not include using PATMOR (Patrol Mortar tubes) launchers, as they were only used by Koevoet operational teams with training presented as part of the Koevoet selection/training course – several Koevoet teams used captured Soviet 61mm Patmor tubes as they were very robust and could successfully launch South African 60mm mortar bombs, but not vice versa.[3]

Those applicants that successfully completed the SAP COIN course were then required to attend a dedicated and specific Koevoet selection course. This would see the officers trained in and tested on;

- Integration with the Ovambo trackers along with very basic terminology.
- A very much enhanced degree of map reading and navigational skills compared to COIN trained cops. This was crucial to successful Koevoet ops. It was incredibly difficult to successfully navigate in a completely flat, featureless landscape. Until the penny dropped whereafter many Koevoet operators could pinpoint their relative positions at the drop of a hat, many times without referring to a map.
- Very basic vehicle maintenance issues, more related to changing wheels and recognising mechanical breakdown issues.
- Soviet firearms and Light and medium machine guns. RPG's and ordnance (B10 recoilless cannons, 122mm rocket launchers etc.) were also included. Landmine awareness and procedures as well as ordnance recognition.
- Additional SA weapons were added to the curriculum such as R4, R5 rifles and CZ 75 pistols.
- 40mm Grenade launchers (Snotnose) – single barrel initially with the Armscor six-shot rotating magazine type coming later.
- Machine guns including 7.62mm FN MAG and .50 cal Browning machine guns. This was not used by SAP at all, only Koevoet. The .50 was the result of continued up-gunning which started with initially liberated HS 20mm cannons and eventually saw South African made G1A1 20mm automatic cannons mounted, flanked by 7.62mm Browning machine guns.
- South African radio sets, TR 48 mostly, with a vast range of programmable HF frequencies and Frequency Hopper capability (although rarely used) were much more extensively trained on to augment the standard training on A53 (FM Ranging between 30-49,975 Mhz, for short range, Line-of-sight Comms) and TR28 (HF with 12 pre-set channels only) types in use by Normal SAP COIN units.[4]

Following the successful completion of selection, the white officers would then be assigned to a call-sign where they would join an experienced team and be required, as the team junior, to rise early in the morning, boil water and serve coffee to 'the group and commanders while they were still in their sleeping bags. In the evening, when a temporary base was established he was again responsible for making the fire and cooking the evening meal.'[5] This until they were deemed 'fit for role' and able to command their own team which could take as long as two years. Critical to which was acceptance by the call-sign's black members. There were certainly occasions when white police officers were sent back to South Africa when the Ovambos refused to work under them.

Koevoet was integrated unit, blacks and whites working together. It was for the white Koeovet officers to prove they could work with the Ovambos and be accepted by the call-sign. Those lacking the requisite personal skills were simply transferred back to the 'States' – South Africa. (Jim Hooper)

For the Ovambos, again, selection and training had progressed considerably since the very early days. Many applicants continued to be illiterate or semi-literate, but it was their tracking skills that Koeovet wanted; their ability to identity a spoor and to mount a pursuit; 'To the Ovambo and the Himba, a spoor was not regarded as merely as a footprint that someone had made in passing. It was a considered part of the spiritual embodiment of the person who made it – a remnant of himself that he had left behind.'[6]

By 1983, the training of the trackers was as flexible as it was practical; 'The sheer number of variables simply did not allow for rigid tactical training regimes.'[7]

Rather Koevoet's operational doctrine and tactical training was aimed at ensuring the trackers were not exposed to undue risk and that the insurgents could be quickly neutralised. Tactics never stand still, in order to be effective they need to evolve and this was certainly the case with Koevoet, where the following key tactics were now taught;

- When information indicated terrs passing, pausing/resting/seen in a specific spot, the trackers from most vehicles will disembark, spread out and search the entire area very slowly and diligently. In this instance the cars would flank relatively wide, keeping as many trackers in sight as possible, failing direct sight, car commanders would constantly relay their relative positions to prevent blue-on-blue mess-ups.
- Car commanders to deliberately drive ahead of the trackers through areas of confinement, that is confluence of kraal hedges where a footpath leads into the confined area, a prime POM-Z spot or similar booby trap. Obviously not when trackers are close enough to be injured in event of triggering an explosion.
- The moment spoor is picked up, all trackers, without exception, will go and visually identify the spoor from the guys on it. They will then disperse to their respective cars to begin 'voorsny' – the practice of leapfrogging with specific intent of picking up spoor ahead.
- If spoor was picked up "On-the-fly", by very sharp and constantly observing trackers whilst driving at speeds of +30Km/h, the car will stop, trackers dismount and verify.
- If possible spoor, all other trackers will visit the known spoor, acquaint themselves accordingly, and then start voorsny.[8]

The use of these tactics and the 'relatively low (very low) turnover of personnel, there was never a situation whereby large numbers of members rotated and were replaced with raw or inexperienced recruits',[9] enabled the teams to deliver an effective COIN utility.

The propagation of tactics and successful procedures was done on a continuous cycle of feedback, analysis and application of lessons learned. Every Wednesday morning, prior to setting out for a week's deployment and of course after the return of the previous week's deployed teams, all group leaders and 2IC's met at Onaimwandi. This was the operational and tactical forum where new information was offered, shared and discussed, changes in tactics (both by Koevoet teams as well as observed terrorist tactics), lessons learnt and related discussions took place. Here then was the place where everything was laid on the table and scrutinised by peers. Lessons learnt was immediately applied. There used to be minimal input by Ops Officers at this point as the team leaders were very much on top of the game and knew exactly the "cause-and-effect" of tactical changes and or adjusted procedures.[10]

The environment certainly determined the way Dreyer's expanded Koevoet operated;

In western Ovamboland, an open area with hard ground difficult for tracking and where people generally supported SWAPO, Koevoet teams spread out and hoped to encounter insurgent spoor by accident. In eastern Ovamboland, with thick bush and less politicised inhabitants, they patrolled and gathered information from locals. Since vehicles could not operate in much of mountainous Kaokoland, Koevoet teams there employed infantry tactics such as observation posts and night ambushes. In sparsely populated Kavango, Koevoet mortared the relatively large insurgent groups operating there to prompt them to split up so that smaller groups or individuals could be tracked with less danger of ambush.[11]

SWAPO's insurgency was aimed at breaking the will of the apartheid government's occupation and in securing liberation. Dreyer knew that an expanded Koevoet working over an ever-increasing geography, would need to mount and prosecute Koevoet operations that were fast, furious and able to generate massive and lethal force. On a fluid 'battlefield' with a high level of manoeuvre, agile mission command was essential. Koevoet's doctrinal approach had evolved to emphasise the need for interoperability – for example, with the SADF and the SAAF – and for rapid manoeuvrability

Simplicity was the key to Koevoet's success – search, locate, close with and neutralise the insurgent enemy through the use of overwhelming lethal force. (Jim Hooper)

achieved through delegated mission command. Dreyer recognised the complexity of COIN – as a set of armed security initiatives aimed at enabling stability and through which legitimate governance could be engendered (not withstanding South Africa's illegal occupation of South West Africa at the time) – but he never saw the need to 'intellectualise' what he saw as a set of simple, integrated, actions; search, locate, close and destroy the insurgent enemy, whilst working to 'protect the local civil population.'

The requirement to mount and prosecute operations was reaffirmed in February 1983 when SWAPO launched another incursion south of the Red Line. A number of PLAN groups sought to move south through Ovamboland and into the heart of the 'triangle of death' en route to the white farming areas. On the 13–14 February 1983, 18 insurgents were killed in a number of contacts and during the period 17–19 February 1983, 92 insurgents from three PLAN groups were killed by Koevoet. This high tempo continued and between 23–25 February 1983, a further three PLAN groups moved south towards the Red Line, east of Ruacana. Koevoet moved to respond and whilst it was certainly securing kills, it was also incurring losses itself as call-sign Zulu Papa was to experience in May.

The team was on a spoor some 45 kilometres south of the cutline. Trackers had been deployed and they were running ahead of the Casspirs as per Koevoet's standard operating procedure. When it was determined that the insurgents were just a few minutes ahead, the Casspirs swung into a double column, other call-signs were alerted to the immediate action and helicopter gunship assistance was requested. One of the white police officers, Constable Botes Botha, was instructed to lead the pursuit and he dismounted from the Casspir to do so. He moved upon the spoor with the trackers and with the two lead Casspirs following up behind.

The insurgents sprung their ambush and Botes dropped to the ground to observe the fall of shot and identify the enemy position. As he did so, an RPG-7 slammed into the tree above him and he was wounded, as was a black warrant officer and two other trackers. This ferocious action saw 11 of the ZP call-sign wounded and evacuated; 'when the contact started, the enemy shot out all three cars on the left. Two were hit on their engines by anti-tank rifle grenades and the third's front differential was knocked out. The Tyres on the Blesbok logisitics vehicle were also shot out. By some miracle no one was killed but there were eleven casevacs.'[12]

On one occasion in May 1983, four Casspirs from call-sign Zulu Whiskey were pursuing a spoor to the south of Ongulumbashe. Two insurgents were spotted trying to make good their escape across a ploughed filed and into the cover of some huts. The call-sign mounted a pursuit and one of the cars headed for a third insurgent who had been spotted. The resultant fightback was observed by a SWAPOL sergeant who noted;

> there was enough time for this man to raise his SKS rifle fitted with a HEAT STRIM grenade and take aim. The next moment there was dust and the sound of an explosion. All I could see was the armour plated glass front of their Casspir shattering into a thousand little pieces. The HEAT STRIM grenade penetrated the Casspir on the left front side,[13]

where it hit and mortally wounded the car commander, Nico Sweigers, and also the Ovambo Warrant Officer, Mr Libius. Two other trackers in the vehicle were also killed.

The Koevoet Casspirs were not invulnerable. Here a Casspir bears witness to an RPG-75 anti-tank grenade that penetrated the armoured glass. The white car commander was killed and the driver wounded. (Jim Hooper)

A damaged Koevoet Casspir is recovered by an SADF Samil-50 Kwevoel Recovery vehicle. Simple repairs could be effected by the call-signs but any major damage would require that the Casspir be recovered to a base workshop. (Jim Hooper)

insurgents through to contact and inevitable neutralisation. The Blesbok boasted a 5-tonne payload capability which was used for transporting ammunition, rations, Casspir/Wolf spare parts and other stores, including five drums of vehicle fuel and additional drums of aviation gas for the supporting SAAF helicopters. There was also a 1,000 litre standalone fuel tank built into the Blesbok;

our cars had a time range of two and a half days (at a constant 4 x 4 Low-Range setting). The drums (5 x 210 Litres, one per car) allowed a single re-fuelling on the evening of the second day of deployment. This then meant a full re-bunker is required mid deployment to replenish both cars and reserve drums. We continued to use Avtur or Jet-A1 in sealed drums for in-field gunship re-fuelling. The logic being the quantity of fuel required for flight exceeded the best case of using a fitted tank. The sealed Jet-A1 drums required immediately prior to usage a leakage check, seal integrity check, an in-date confirmation and a final visual check for contaminants once opened which satisfied the criteria for use.[14]

Whilst better equipment and improved access to logistic support readied Koevoet to sustain operations, improved signals equipment allowed for better command and coordination. Koevoet was scaled with the South African TR series of equipment including the TR48 radio (an HF system with a Frequency Hopper capability), the A53 (FM Ranging between 30-49,975 Mhz, for short range, line-of-sight Comms) and the TR28 (HF with 12 pre-set channels only) which was commonly used by the SAP and SWAPOL. On operations

Koevoet could ill afford an increasing casualty count and so Dreyer had to continuously innovate to ensure that the COIN essentials of protection, firepower and mobility were furthered. The development and issue of the Wolf Turbo, designed and manufactured locally in Namibia, went some way to ensure Koevoet maintained the advantage. This along with the development of the Blesbok mine-protected logistics vehicle and the Duiker fuel bowser gave Koevoet significant additional protection and mobility. The practice of mounting heavier gun combinations on the Casspirs and Wolfs afforded greater firepower. This was augmented in some instances, with the addition of light mortars affixed to a base plate on the vehicle.

Both the Blesbok and Duiker were to give Dreyer's call-signs the additional flexibility they needed to stay on spoor and track the

Koevoet generally operated a single radio net with strict radio discipline which meant everyone had, at all times, situational awareness of THE ENTIRE OPERATIONAL AREA AS OPERATED BY KOEVOET! This is anathema to military commanders, but for Koevoet command structure it developed that way and continued successes proved it to be the only way to go. Most Koevoet command and 2IC cars had all three types of radio fitted, whilst cars 3 and 4 as well as Blesbok only had the A53 and TR28 as standard. In theory any car could immediately take over as command car if the command car radios were not functioning of course with limited long range abilities. For less important team specific messages, a different frequency would be called for so as not to impede on the operational frequency. Most teams expeditiously listened in on such discussions for no other reason to appease their inherent enquiring mindedness!

This meant any team leader recognizing a better application of his team's capabilities could offer it at any moment subject to approval from the boss (Or sneak in closer …!) Delay the approval and then sort of 'appear' on the scene so to speak![15]

A well-run control room also added to effective command and signals. Dreyer was especially demanding of his Operations Officers and only the best would do. Captain John Adam was one of Koevoet's early 'Op Cell Officers'; 'Intensely patriotic and loyal, particularly to those under his command, he was the catalyst in changing the unit from an intelligence operation into the counter insurgency force that was to become, thanks to his innovation and leadership, so successful.'[16]

Pictured in the rough terrain of Kaokoland, the Wolf Turbo was a significant addition to the Koevoet inventory. (Jim Hooper)

Dreyer pictured in a Koevoet Operations Room. Effective command, control and communication was essential if Koevoet were to keep SWAPO and PLAN at bay. (Jim Hooper)

Through the architecture of an effective signals capability, competent Operations Officers, experienced call-sign leaders and car commanders, Koevoet was able to exercise good command and coordination right down to the lowest level, that of the tracker, where the judicious use of field signals often led to direct contact with the insurgents;

Over time, many team-specific personal tactics developed. Many a car commander recognized minute signals from trackers on the spoor and rapidly adjusted position relative to the trackers or informed other cars accordingly without a further word from the ground. A rapid four-fingered point of the lead trackers hand may shift the entire teams focus and direction as well as the follow-up speed. There can never be a rule book for this. It developed through years of experience, mutual respect and recognition of masters at work.[17]

Four years in and Koevoet was changing. Its senior leadership was being rotated back to South Africa, new white officers were joining the ever-expanding number of teams and its operational procedures were being continuously reviewed to ensure success against SWAPO. Its doctrinal approach continued to evolve such that it was now an, enhanced, eight-part – as opposed to four – construct. Namely;

- The continued and ongoing execution of investigative police work to secure intelligence from the community

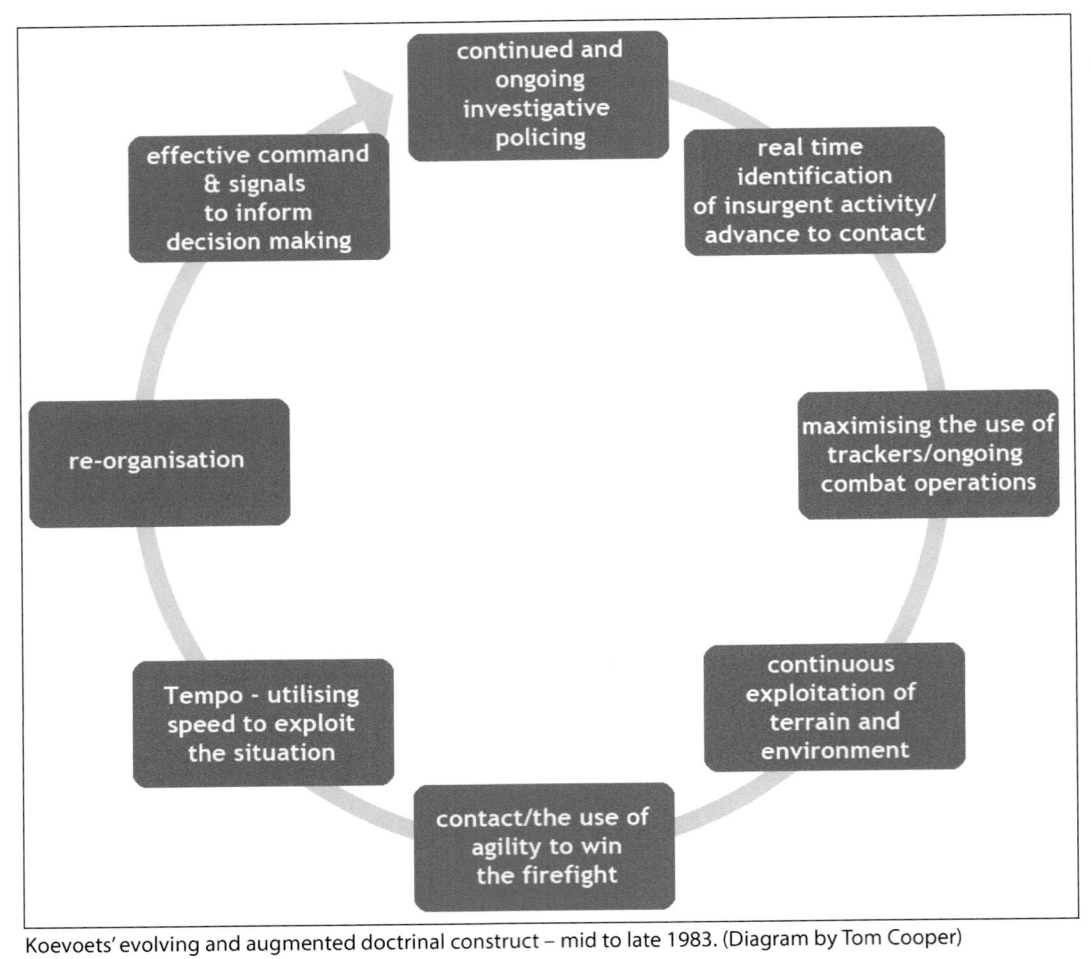

Koevoets' evolving and augmented doctrinal construct – mid to late 1983. (Diagram by Tom Cooper)

- From intelligence secured, the accurate and real-time identification of possible insurgent groups or insurgent activity, utilising information superiority to inform quality decision making and precise engagement with the insurgents – accelerating the advance to contact
- Maximising the use of trackers who are able to use their tracking skills, senses, local knowledge of the terrain and population to process information and effect an ongoing combat appreciation as they close with the enemy
- Continuous exploitation of terrain and environment – no matter how difficult to negotiate (eg. the rocky mountains of Kaokoland) – leaving no space for SWAPO to hide or harbour within
- Upon contact, ascertaining the existence of insurgents, confirming their identity, numbers and strengths; aggressive search and destroy action to neutralise the

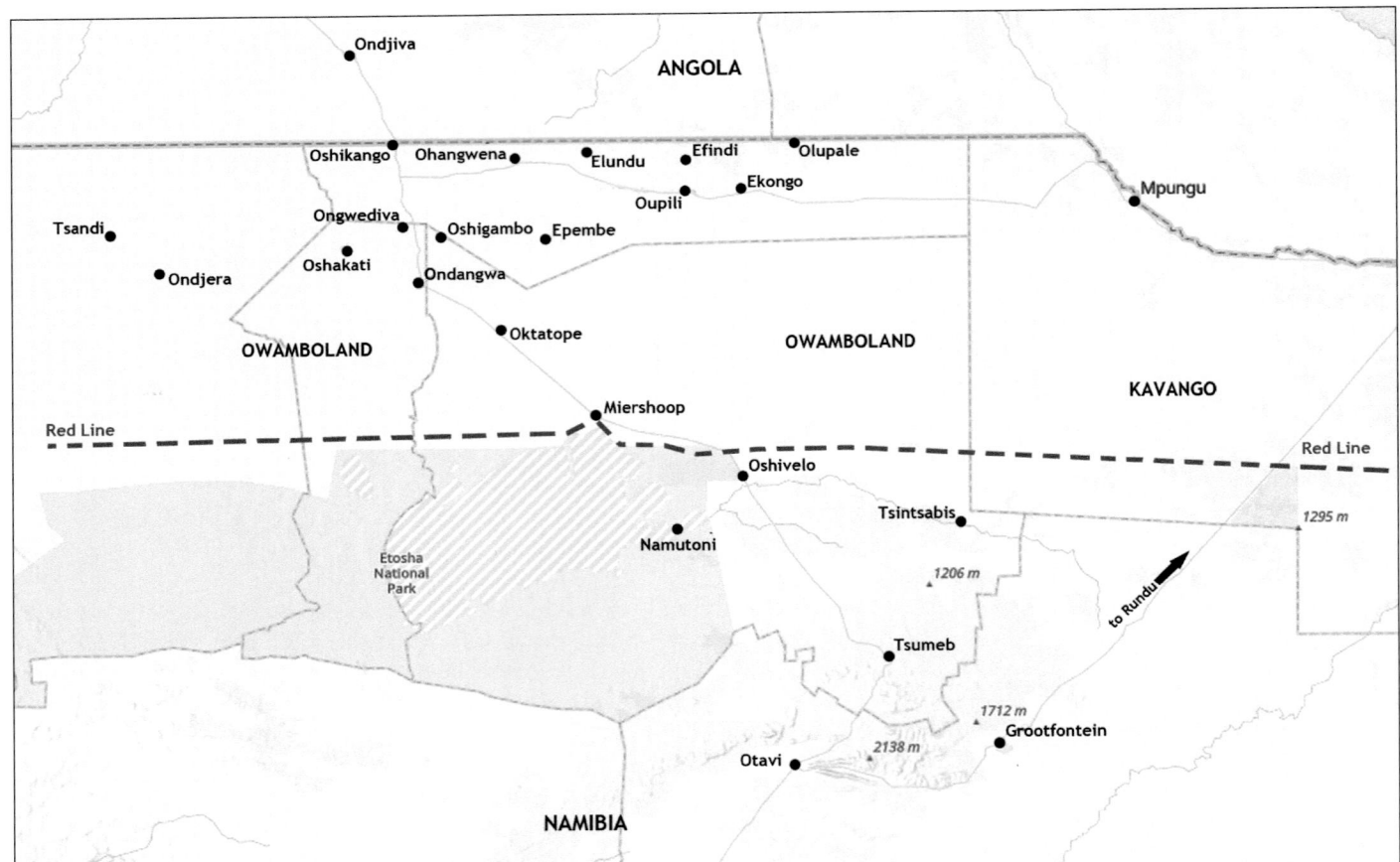

The 'Red Line' or 'Mangeti' stretched right across Namibia from the eastern edge of Ovamboland to the west of Kavango and the Botswana border. (Map by Tom Cooper)

insurgent threat; utilising the call-sign's protection, mobility and firepower to best effect
- The maintenance of tempo – utilising speed to exploit a situation or contact to its full lethal extent; this being a combination of speed, responsiveness and agility aimed at striking enemy forces at a critical juncture, again and again – i.e. having completed one action, the immediate mounting of the next
- Having won the action, re-organisation. Confirming numbers and identity of the dead, processing captives, securing intelligence and where appropriate, 'turning' insurgents to join Koevoet
- The use of effective command and signals to ensure good, practical, dialogue on operations which informed leadership and decision making, enhanced 'productivity' and, thereby, maintained high morale

Pictured from a Koevoet Casspir, an SADF Ratel 90 moves at speed along a tarred road. The Ratel IFV series were superbly effective during the Border War but surprisingly vulnerable to RPG attacks. The SADF experienced a number of losses. (Jim Hooper)

Koevoet trackers seek to confirm a spoor. PLAN fighters became adept at anti-tracking, using a range of means to throw their pursuers off track including the laying of false spoors. (Jim Hooper)

This construct was put to good use mid to late 1983 as Koevoet worked to counter the increasing SWAPO infiltration into both Ovamboland and the Kavango. As another rainy season approached, it was obvious that the 'summer games' were about to re-commence. In December 1983, intelligence suggested that a large-scale infiltration was due. In order to deny SWAPO the ability to act, the SADF mounted an offensive operation titled Operation Askari. This was designed to strike at, and neutralise, the SWAPO concentrations in southern Angola and the FAPLA forces that were harbouring them. Askari was also aimed at neutralising the increasingly sophisticated air defence systems the Angolans had deployed to counter South African air activity. Without air superiority, the South Africans would obviously struggle to contain the insurgency.

Askari was opened by SAAF air suppression strikes which were then followed by SADF battlegroup ground assaults on the towns of Cuvelai, Mulundo, Quiteve, Cahama and Caiundo. The response was fierce with the South Africans having to contend with FAPLA armour in the form of T55 tanks, one of which destroyed a Ratel IFV in which six SADF soldiers were killed. Cuban forces also mobilised to support SWAPO forces in Cuvelai which, after fierce street fighting, was eventually captured and held by the SADF, the fleeing SWAPO, PLAN and FAPLA forces being harassed by 32 Battalion as they effected their retreat.

Yet still the insurgents came and Koevoet continued to identify, pursue, track and neutralise, despite the ever-increasing efforts by SWAPO and PLAN to counter-track and evade the call-signs. Such counter-tracking would involve the insurgents breaking off track and changing their footwear or doubling back on the spoor that had been laid, to throw off their pursuers. Alternatively, leaving a false spoor by walking backwards over soft ground so as to confuse and disorientate. On other occasions, the noise of the Casspir engines would alert the insurgents who would then scatter or evade.

During one pursuit in the Kavango, call-signs Zulu Delta and Zulu Echo had been on spoor for six days, tracking two insurgents. These insurgents were managing to evade the following cars and it was clear to the car commanders that they were being alerted by the sound of the vehicles;

> ... on the seventh day (of the pursuit), they ordered the Casspirs to withdraw to give the impression the spoor had been lost and the chase abandoned. With two teams of ten trackers each, (they) set off on foot with only personal weapons, a minimum of equipment and a backpack radio. They followed the spoor for two kilometres before they came upon the two insurgents listening to a portable radio and relaxing under a tree. It was clear they believed Koevoet had called off the hunt. Unfortunately for them, they didn't even have time to bring their AKs to bear before they died in a hail of bullets.[18]

Contacts would often take the form of hasty ambushes laid to kill and neutralise pursuing Koeovet call-signs. The 'L-shaped' ambush was a common method which saw insurgents seek to hit the dismounted trackers and Casspir vehicles from two sides. Ordinarily, the Koevoet call-signs would quickly determine if the insurgents had broken off track to lay an ambush; the break in stride and the disrupted spoor being evident that the insurgents had doubled back on themselves or elsewhere. Call-sign leaders or car commanders would invariably pull back the dismounted trackers to the vehicles to ensure their protection and utilise the firepower mounted upon the Casspirs for force protection. This in addition to calling in SAAF gunship assets, if available, or other call-signs so as to maximise the available firepower.

The usual response to any ambush was to drive through the killing zone at speed laying down the maximum firepower possible and using the weight of the vehicles to run over, circle and neutralise the insurgents. Once the firefight had been judged to have been won and no further resistance detected, the trackers would dismount to conduct a sweep for the dead, wounded and those who may have surrounded, recovering weapons, equipment and documents in the process.

There is no denying that many SWAPO ambushes were deadly effective and armed with man-portable anti-tank weapons, namely anti-tank mines that could be quickly laid and RPG-7 grenade launchers with armour piercing capabilities, the insurgents were readily able to destroy a Casspir and Koevoet losses certainly occurred;

> At approximately 2.00pm our team and one another drove into a L shaped ambush. For what felt like ten minutes but in reality it only lasted a couple of minutes, there was a lot of gunfire, and mortar bombs were falling all around us along with the unmistakable sound of RPG-7s being fired. I shoved my rifle through a gun port and shot at something I could not see. Scared? Oh yeah!
>
> We had driven into a group of about eighty SWAPO terrorists at a forward base camp where even trenches had been dug. One of the APCs had taken the brunt of the initial salvo of RPG-7s, and had been hit three times. We came across the Casspir smouldering from the intense heat caused by the rockets. Looking inside I saw three of our black colleagues lying in various positions, the one's face had been shot away and the other two were a bloody mess. Nearby we found our only kill: one SWAPO terrorist dressed in rice fleck camouflage.[19]

8

1984 – The Lusaka Accord: Koevoet Stands Firm

Operation Askari was a military success which succeeded in both blunting the insurgency and leveraging an unexpected political consequence. As a result of pressure from the Americans, the South Africans were forced to consider a negotiated settlement with the Angolans. The ongoing War of Liberation was becoming a strain for Angola who were having to bear the increasing political, military and economic cost of having SWAPO and PLAN bases on its soil. The war was proving a financial drain and causing civil disquiet. But by the same token, Pretoria was also struggling. The COIN effort was costly and attracting condemnation including international sanctions which were damaging. The increasing casualty rate was also difficult to justify. The domestic anti-war movement was picking up apace and an end conscription campaign was gaining momentum. Founded in 1983, the End Conscription Campaign (ECC) sought to bring an end to conscription and to oppose the presence of the SADF in Namibia. The ECC used a variety of media to criticise the South African government's approach to conscription and amongst many middle class whites, was to create angst and fear. Few wanted their sons returning home to the 'States' in body-bags.

Talks were convened in Lusaka, Zambia, where the South Africans and Angolans met to determine a ceasefire agreement. In summary, the South Africans were prepared to withdraw their forces from Angola, so long as FAPLA, SWAPO and the Cubans did the same. In response, Angola indicated that it would use all means possible to ensure SWAPO respected the proposed agreement but, in return, it wanted an end to South African support for UNITA.

South Africa's combat aims had been to deny SWAPO and PLAN the ability to use Angola as a launch platform for insurgent activity into Namibia. If Angola were to curtail SWAPO's adventurism, then the SADF would have realised and fulfilled its mission objective. To this end, the Pretoria judged the agreement acceptable, and the Lusaka Accords were signed in February 1984 resulting in a formal ceasefire declaration between Angola and South Africa. The agreement required Pretoria to withdraw all its troops and for FAPLA to move in and occupy the former South African positions so as to deny ground to SWAPO and PLAN. All of this to be overseen by a Joint Monitoring Commissioning (JMC) which was to comprise South African and Angolan observers.

In February 1984, the JMC headquarters was established at Cuvelai from where monitoring patrols would be conducted. Both the Bushman 101 Battalion and 32 Battalion were tasked to work with FAPLA and right from the start, the joint patrols encountered

Koevoet's Use and Application of Intelligence

Koevoet's acquisition, analysis and application of intelligence was second to none. Recruiting from the local population afforded Dreyer and his leadership unrivalled access to language skills and local knowledge. The use of turned fighters enabled Koevoet to secure ready information on SWAPO & PLAN's military leadership, organisation, intentions, resilience and motivations.

Taken together this approach allowed Koevoet to develop a bottom-up flow of intelligence information which informed the planning and execution of COIN activities. This flow being augmented regularly with information secured by the SAP, SWAPOL and SADF so that a full intelligence picture could be detailed. Koevoet's use of informers was key to ensuring the collection of quality Human Intelligence (HUMINT). The informers received low-level training in how to secure intelligence material from noted individuals, documents and other media.

More often than not, HUMINT was passed readily to the Koevoet teams as they patrolled kraals and engaged the local population. This, in effect, being reconnaissance by conversation with village elders and children often keen to impart information; elders because they wanted to keep their kraals and family/village members safe; children because they are naturally inquisitive and always happy to reveal all. Hence, the local population inadvertently became the 'eyes and ears' of Koevoet, delivering real-time intelligence to the call-signs.

The challenge to the teams was how to determine what intelligence was useful and what was simply a rumour, planted information or plainly incorrect. Fortunately, the trackers with their local knowledge and perspective were able to quicky sift and act on the information received.

In some instances, Koevoet would use covert standing patrols as a surveillance tool. Placed to gather information on a particular kraal or geographical feature, and cross referenced with HUMINT and any other intelligence material – aerial photographs, signals intelligence (SIGINT) – the teams would be able to secure content that allowed Koevoet's leadership to determine where and how best to counter SWAPO's intentions.

This approach has persisted through until today where, for example, in Afghanistan and Mali, COIN forces have invested significantly in the acquisition and analysis of HUMINT, to the extent that HUMINT cells are deployed across the COIN force and the use of civilian contractors, working as interpreters and interrogators, is normalised. This reinforcing, as per the Koevoet experience, the critical need to develop an all-source intelligence perspective that informs commanders as to the insurgent intent.

Koevoet trackers removes weapons, equipment and documents from a dead insurgent. PLAN's operational security or 'OPSEC' was surprisingly poor. Many of the fighters carried notebooks and documentation that yielded a considerable amount of useful intelligence. (Jim Hooper)

insurgents. A number of skirmishes resulted and it was evident that SWAPO and PLAN were still on the ground in southern Angola because no one sought to include SWAPO in the ceasefire agreement and to appraise them of the role of the JMC. Hence, with the South Africans withdrawn, SWAPO took the opportunity to brazenly consolidate its presence in areas controlled by FAPLA, who simply looked the other way and denied any knowledge of such activity. There was also a further tension in that the South Africans did little to compartmentalise UNITA as Luanda had requested. With regard to the Cubans, they were little impacted upon by the Accord as their operational bases were further to the north, however, it was noted that they took the opportunity to reinforce their conventional forces. Right from the start, the Accord was in obvious disarray and whilst the JMC continued to meet, it was clear that parties to the agreement had no intention of adhering to the detail within. SWAPO continued to infiltrate into Angola and the SADF continued to conduct reconnaissance activity to search for and identify insurgent bases.

However, dialogue was to continue and in May 1984, talks were convened in Windhoek by the esteemed Zambian leader, President Kaunda, and the Namibian Administrator General, Willie van Niekerk. This Multi-Party Conference (MPC) sought to secure a peace settlement, but SWAPO refused to engage despite a growing sense that a resolution was needed. With no sign of any traction with SWAPO, the MPC requested that the South African government assemble a transitional government to determine a road map for, and to, independence.

There was now a real desire to see a political solution to the War of Liberation, but for Koevoet, the operational tempo was as high as ever. By the middle of 1984, SWAPO's insurgent intentions were as robust as they had ever been, its leadership, insurgents and PLAN fighters committed to the liberation effort as the insurgency began to move from that of 'strategic defensive', to one of 'strategic stalemate.'

From the founding of Koevoet in 1979 to the time of the MPC, SWAPO had been operating in 'strategic defensive mode.' This given that the South Africans possessed superior strength what with the SADF, the SWATF, SAP and SWAPOL working in concert to effect COIN operations against a numerically inferior and equipped capability. Notwithstanding that this was a liberation and insurgent movement that was able to sow discontent amongst the civil population, infiltrate local civil society infrastructures and conduct subversive activity; assassinating key civic personalities, intimidating the population, mounting hit and run attacks against the security forces.

By mid-1984, the South Africans and SWAPO had moved from strategic defensive mode into a 'strategic stalemate.' SWAPO and PLAN had increased their strength in numbers, had improved their operational effectiveness as a result of training from their various foreign sponsors, were equipped with plentiful weapons and had developed a sophisticated network of bases from which to launch insurgent activities. They were also less fearful of the South Africans who, in order to maintain the insurgency at a point of equity, were having to deploy more forces, and to continue to 'Namibiase' the war through the employment of more locally recruited assets.

For Dreyer, the stalemate required Koevoet to ensure an intensity of effort that, in order to maintain the 'legitimacy' of the South African government and to counter the insurgency; reassured the local population and guaranteed their security. One that continued to secure intelligence – particularly HUMINT – with which to ascertain SWAPO intentions and, through the execution of dedicated and specific COIN operations, neutralise the insurgents.

At an operational and call-sign level there was no let up. Deployed to the Kavango, call-sign Zulu 4 Sierra mounted pursuits to the north of the Kavango, across a geography that ranged from Namungundo in the south of the Kavango to Nepara and Ncaute in the north. Tasked to track a spoor identified by a kraal elder, the call-sign moved into a well-rehearsed routine;

Two tracks going west. Hendrik Engelbrecht, Clemens Kamberuka and Lukas Koen confer. We have a plan. Henrik asks 12 trackers to follow on foot. The Casspirs turn around and proceed in the opposite direction. It is a quiet follow-up on tracks that are four hours old. The follow-up is fast and we catch up quickly. There is a small hill in front of us and we climb it to see if we can spot them. While climbing the hill, we and the insurgents see each other simultaneously. They start running but they are too far away for us to catch them. Plans change. We call the cars. Following them on foot does not work well today. And now they know we are tracking them. The element of surprise is gone.[1]

Zulu 4 Sierra was unable to close with and neutralise the insurgents on this occasion but when it did, it was quick to announce its success. Koevoet call-signs would frequently display the clothing and equipment of neutralised insurgents. With Sisingi Kamongo's Zulu 4 Sierra this would involve the flying of red flags on sticks or radio aerials and the hoisting of insurgent camouflage garments;

After every contact we would fasten a red flag to a stick on the command car. We would take the insurgents' clothes and fasten them to the sticks as well. The dead insurgents would be strapped to the mudguards of the cars. Then we would drive past the huts and kraals, brandishing the AKs, SKKs and RPGs above our heads on the top of the Casspirs.

There could be no doubt as to who we had shot. Definitely not innocents. It would be to show the SWAPO sympathisers that they too were not immune to death.[2]

Identifying the dead insurgents was critical to Koeovet as it worked to maintain the intelligence picture as to who was who in the SWAPO and PLAN orbat, what operations were planned, what weapon caches were located where and what munitions they comprised? Through the acquisition of good quality field intelligence and HUMINT, effective COIN operations can be planned and executed.

Sometimes bodies would be identified in the field from notebooks or other material that the insurgent was carrying. On other occasions, Dreyer would require the call-signs to organise for the despatch of the dead to Oshakati or another Koevoet base for identification. Sometimes helicopters would be assigned to the tasking. After one expanse contact which saw several call-signs engage a large group of insurgents;

Dreyer said he wanted all the bodies in Oshakati and said he would be sending Super Frelons to fetch them. This he did. We had to collect all these messy bodies spread over a distance of more than two kilometres. The Ovambos don't like handling dead bodies and would only assist in dragging them to a central point. We had to put all these dead bodies in body-bags. Luckily at that time AIDS was not an issue. All these bodies were in uniform from head to toe.[3]

On other occasions, the bodies would be strapped, controversially, to the mudguards or wheel arches of the Casspirs, principally, because there was no other place to carry the dead. The fighting compartment in a Casspir is a small and chaotic place at best. Add the trackers, their weapons, ammunition, water and rations, then there is no place to lay a body that has experienced penetrating and possibly amputating gunshot trauma; leaking blood, faeces and tissue matter and with the additional risk of HIV or Hepatitis infection.

Given that the Ovambos did not like handling the dead – this as a result of their particular and cultural approach to death, a fusion of tribal belief and modernist Christianity drawn from the teachings of Finnish missionaries – they would simply affix the body to the outside of the vehicle by the quickest means. As Sisingi Kamongo remarked to the author in London in 2011, this was not a question of ghoulish display, but rather one of transporting the remains for identification. Indeed, once the bodies had been identified, they would invariably be buried in mass graves. Evidence of such is the existence of a number of contemporary photographs that document the burial of PLAN fighters in mass graves at Uupindi, west of Oshakati.

In May 1984, 30 PLAN fighters infiltrated into the area around Otjiboronbonga in Kaokoland. Led by an assertive commander named 'Soviet', this PLAN unit mounted reconnaissance patrols and conducted observation serials on the small SADF base at Etengwa. Manned by just one army platoon from 102 Battalion, the Etenga base was sited to dominate the southern bank of the Cunene River and provide a COIN presence out to Otjiboronbonga in the west.

Soviet planned to launch a stand-off mortar attack on the base and so had his fighters lay anti-tank mines on the only approaching access road, so that any reinforcing SADF elements despatched from the nearby Okangwati base would be neutralised.

Early on the morning of 24 May, Soviet initiated the mortar attack which saw 82mm and 60mm mortars deployed along with anti-tank and rifle grenades. The army platoon mounted a spirited defence with the platoon medic earning an Honorus Crux for exposing himself to the enemy action as he positioned himself to return fire, wounding two insurgents in the process. However, the tented camp was destroyed, and the PLAN group made good their escape. The SADF despatched reinforcements from Okangwati – the most north-westerly base in Namibia and nestling at the foot of the Zebra mountains – which immediately hit the landmines laid by the PLAN group though, fortunately, there were no casualties. The army were too small in number to mount a follow-up and so the Koevoet calls-signs in Opuwo were called in. Three call-signs were deployed and at the first available opportunity, they identified and picked up the blood spoor left by the two wounded insurgents which was seen to be moving towards Otjiboronbonga. The call-signs utilised their well-rehearsed tactics to mount a classic Koevoet pursuit. As always;

The Koevoet trackers exhibited immense physical fitness and stamina; pursuits would often last for days on end, the trackers on the ground rotated between those mounted on the vehicles. (Jim Hooper)

- Trackers deployed on the ground lightly armed with their R5 personal weapons and chest webbing for the carriage of ammunition
- The Casspirs followed up from the rear, in single file, behind the trackers, readied, to move left and right onto the flanks should the insurgents be spotted or, if in open ground, the vehicles would, usually, be deployed line abreast
- All gun systems made ready to direct lethal firepower onto the insurgents
- Signals links to the SAAF active and open, so that aviation assets could be called upon

The speed at which the Koevoet teams could move was fast, the trackers possessing incredible fitness and stamina. Invariably, the trackers on the ground would pursue the spoor for as long and as fast as they could, before the lead Casspir would pick them up and fresh trackers would jump down to continue the pursuit. In this manner the trackers would leapfrog over each other to maintain the momentum. Sometimes the Casspirs would jump ahead to try and cut off the fleeing insurgents or simply to close the gap. Tracking the Koevoet way was certainly an art and great distances were covered;

… sometimes the trackers were running so fast it was hard to keep up, and sometimes the pace slowed to a crawl, when it was apparent that the quarry were applying anti-tracking drills, going slowly after changing direction, lightly sweeping their footprints with leafed branches. When they changed direction, the trackers sometimes overran the spoor and would have to turn back and do a 360 of the area until one of them would pick up the tracks, leading in a new direction.[4]

As the trackers moved closer to the insurgents, the pace would increase;

With time and experience you could later determine more or less how far you are behind the terrs. When the spoor became paife – imminent – it would break into short steps of running and then anti-track again. Whenever the terrs ran you could be very close on their heels or they could lay and wait in ambush for you. However, forty people on a spoor with forty different adrenaline levels, also makes it a bit complicated when getting to paife![5]

In this instance at Etengwa, the rocky terrain of the Kaokoland was proving impassible to the Casspirs and so the SAAF was called in to assist;

> One stick took the spoor and the other two leapfrogged ahead by Puma (helicopter) for two or three kilometres. The distances varied depending on the terrain and whether the spoor twisted and turned or went straight. When a leapfrogging team found the spoor they followed it while the Puma returned to pick up the first stick and leapfrog thar ahead, and so forth.[6]

The pursuit was maintained for several days with the aircraft and teams crossing into southern Angola, but despite all efforts, on this occasion, the insurgents got away.

Koevoet Bases

During a previous southern African COIN campaign, the British sought to dominate the ground by building a network of fortifications. The Boer War saw Kitchener lay out a network of forts and blockhouses that were designed to monitor Boer movements and to ensure that ground that had been 'ethnically cleansed', remained as such. Initially sited to prevent against the destruction of railway tracks by Boer Commando forces, the forts were placed strategically so that they linked up to form a series of 'stop lines.'

The forts were built to a series of uniform designs and most were three storeys in height. The top floor for observation and the mounting of machine guns. British forces would occupy these forts – or blockhouses – and conduct patrols from them. The duty was tedious and dull, with the Boers simply moving around the forts to avoid detection. The British repeated the same in Northern Ireland where, during the course of Operation Banner, it built a network of 12 hilltop forts across South Armagh. As with the Boer War, the aim being to strengthen the COIN effort by affording platforms that allow for the observation of insurgent activity.

For Koevoet there were no concrete blockhouses or corrugated iron 'Golf' watchtowers. Dreyer's men dominated the ground by being mobile. Overnight halts saw the teams draw up their Casspirs into all round defence. Occasionally the teams would establish 'Tydelike Basis', Afrikaans for a 'temporary base' (TB) but this would be rare as the paramount need was to be mobile in pursuit of SWAPO insurgents and PLAN fighters. The defensive routine at night was minimal, ponchos would be strung, up sleeping bags laid out and cooking fires permitted. The tactical view was that insurgents would not attack a Koevoet formation at night. In addition: 'they'd need to have a force already near a TB, the location of which was impossible to predict, and enough men to take on up to 40 battle hardened Koevoet operators – twice that number if two teams shared a TB.'[7]

A welcome evening meal is prepared at a Koevoet TB. (Jim Hooper)

A call-sign awakens in its TB; Coffee and ProNutro is readied for breakfast. (Jim Hooper)

In order to mount a rapid pursuit and to ensure operations could be sustained, the Koevoet teams would pack their vehicles with ammunition, water and rations. These stocks would be augmented by those carried in the Blesbok armoured supply vehicles which would also carry fuel, oil and lubricants for the Casspirs, along with drums of aviation spirit for use by the SAAF helicopters. If circumstances required, the teams would often visit SADF bases to resupply;

> Koevoet teams often visited army bases out of necessity. There were enough supplies on the Blesbok for a week out on patrol, but when things developed differently the supplies were usually used up more quickly than was anticipated: diesel, helicopter fuel, water, ammunition, rat packs. Sometimes circumstances developed that caused us to stay in the field longer. We often had to leave lightly wounded or ill members at the sick bay of an army base.[8]

The Koevoet teams sought to maximise their time in the field so that they could move quickly to mount pursuits and close with the enemy. Koevoet operations were renowned for moving from that of considered engagement with the community, the gathering of intelligence, interpretation and analysis, to armed and lethal pursuit in a matter of moments;

> … we had stopped at one more kraal. The trackers walked to the log palisade and began questioning the head of the family. The conversation became animated the farmer gesturing angrily from inside the enclosure. Watching the scene I thought his anger was directed at us. I couldn't have been more mistaken. One of the trackers shouted to Toit. Two insurgents had come the night before and taken a goat without paying for it. The farmer wasn't sure which way they had gone, but he thought to the east, pointing and snapping his fingers.
>
> Toit was reaching for the handset when Attie's voice crackled over the radio. His trackers had found seven spoor less than a mile east of us. The tracks were only two or three hours old. The change in everyone was immediate, an electric energy sparking through the group. Minutes later we rendezvoused with Zulu Uniform. The trackers jumped off the cars with their stubby assault rifles, paused to chamber rounds, then ran to join those already on the trail. The hunt has begun.[9]

By now, late 1984, Koevoet was heading to the end of its expansionist phase. From an original four call-signs in 1978 it now boasted 20 operating out of the Oshakati headquarters base and its four other satellite bases – Ondangwa, Ongwediva, Rundu and Opuwa. It had developed a recruitment, training and logistics capability such that Koevoet was very much a standalone concern and one that, with its integrated information gathering and combat functionality, was able to move seamlessly from investigative policing to warfighting. During the first five years of its existence, Koevoet had effectively demonstrated the utility of its, now, eight-part COIN construct which sought to neutralise the SWAPO insurgents and PLAN fighters in order to ensure the maintenance of civil security as required by the South African government and once secured, assign primacy for policing to the SAP and SWAPOL. Hence, Koevoet's success was partly due to its ability to transit from policing to warfighting and back, such as the insurgency demanded. Indeed, there were many instances when Koevoet declared an area to be free from SWAPO, only to have the insurgents re-emerge. This would then mean the call-signs would have to move back to neutralise the threat.

The very essence of COIN is the assembly and delivery of an integrated military, paramilitary, political, economic and civil society response to the insurgent threat. This has been seen in recent years in Northern Ireland, Iraq and Afghanistan where expanse efforts have been made to provide civil security, a functioning state and economic opportunity, so as to reduce attraction to the insurgent or liberation cause. In Northern Ireland, it can be argued that the British COIN effort was a success given that the 1998 Good Friday Agreement (GFA) saw the tabling of a multi-party agreement that ended most of the violence of the Troubles. Yet the British government still maintains a discreet COIN effort through its existing security services, police and military apparatus. This being aimed at preventing any resurgent nationalist insurgency. In Iraq and Afghanistan the COIN effort is largely judged to have failed and, in the case of Afghanistan in 2022, spectacularly so.

In Namibia, the South African COIN strategy and Koevoet's role in the execution of that strategy, to the end of 1984, was broadly successful in that;

- The occupying South African government, the SADF, the SAP, the SWATF and SWAPOL worked together to tackle SWAPO. Joint force structure and force application planning worked well (generally speaking, as there were some SADF senior ranks who were jealous of or resented Koevoet).
- SWAPO was, on the whole, denied the opportunity to establish bases in Namibia and the South Africans were not afraid to mount 'externals' into Angola to neutralise SWAPO and PLAN concentrations.
- Infiltration into Namibia was difficult with the pattern of major infiltrations – that is the Summer Games – and the routes to be taken, known to the South Africans who could then prepare and respond accordingly.
- The South Africans initiated COIN operations from areas of strength such as Oshakati, Rundu and Ondangua and Opuwu, reaching out into the local population to support and assure; through which ground could be denied to SWAPO or be retaken if SWAPO were to reappear.
- There were sustained efforts to win hearts and minds or 'WHAM', as it was known, through the dissemination of anti-SWAPO propaganda. Whilst there was universal and obvious hatred amongst the civil population of the South African's *petty* apartheid; messaging delivered by the indigenous trackers of Koevoet which sought to counter SWAPO's ideology and mission – that the South African occupation was better than a Marxist state – was occasionally well received.

Furthermore, the South Africans framed their COIN response into a three-part, sequential, equation that looked to combine policing and warfighting with efforts to deliver a stable civil society platform that would reduce the appeal of SWAPO's cause. The three parts being;

Executive Action to Halt the Insurgency

Through the raising and deployment of COIN forces such as Koevoet, tasked to secure intelligence with which to identify the insurgents and to inform subsequent offensive operations aimed at neutralising SWAPO and PLAN, all of which whilst protecting and supporting the civil population.

Effecting Stability

Through civil society stabilising, investigative policing and warfighting activities that utilise all lines of operation to counter the insurgents. This to achieve a status where the civil population is protected, assured and enabled to go about its usual business. This in turn allowing for the greater acquisition of field intelligence and HUMINT which informs the ongoing planning and execution of Koevoet operations; utilising initiative to search for and neutralise the enemy.

Transition to Self-Sufficiency

In essence, the move away from a COIN position to one where the insurgency has been neutralised and security has been assigned to the civil state and the police.

Key to ensuring the success of this equation was the South African use of Lines of Operation (LOs). These lines being varying aspects of the COIN operation tabled into one ready reckoner or dashboard for quick reference and accessible decision making; informed decision making which clarifies and affirms the purpose of the COIN mission.

In the dashboard detailed, each of the LOs detailed are pathways through which the South African government sought to counter SWAPO: offensive combat operations; the deployment of security forces to secure the ground; the delivery of essential services – access to health, education and employment; good functioning governance; progressive and sustained economic development.

These LOs cross-referenced and success in one leveraged others. Through prioritisation, the South Africans were able to determine where to apply focus and effort – for example, the simultaneous deployment of Koevoet to prosecute warfighting, whilst SADF army teachers were assigned to teach disabled children in a local school. This in turn, allowing the civil population the security to participate in gainful employment which stimulates the economy and creates local wealth; wealth which fosters resilience and reduces the desire to support the liberation movement.

Working to its eight-part doctrinal construct, Dreyer's Koevoet was part of a joint force structure that, as mentioned previously, generally worked well, though there were times when elements of the SADF accused Koevoet of monitoring its signals traffic so that its call-signs could identify pursuits where they could leap ahead to the point of contact and secure the kill. Indeed, there were some who believed that this was Koevoet's principal and reckless way of working – let others do the tracking until that point when Koeovet was ready to strike and, thereby, take the credit for a successful operation.

A successful contact would sometimes see the payment of 'head money';

> ... whether our contact was dead or alive, the number of rifles, landmines, mortar pipes, mortars, uniforms etc. recovered, was paid for. But all the money was divided up among the team members and sometimes among the members of other teams who had helped. It was still very little. The most money I ever got was R370 ($50) when we found a B10 cannon and rounds. More often than not it was just R10 or R20 per contact. We were robbed by the police.[10]

The payment of head money or 'kopgeld' was an accepted Koeovet norm; 'A R1,000 for a kill, R2,000 for a prisoner. And there's a scale for weapons that goes from R250 for an AK47, up to R10,000 for a SAM-7. Which only goes to the trackers, by the way. Not much when you divide it between 40 to 45 men.'[11]

There were some who challenged Koevoet's aggressive approach and its pursuit of kopgeld including the Chief of the SADF, General Johannes Geldenhuys, who was emphatic in his criticism; 'Koevoet would, for example, go into an area, clean it up, then collect the bodies and drag them through town behind their vehicles. Obviously this kind of action upset the local population greatly and we'd find we were suddenly getting no more cooperation from the locals.'[12]

PLAN naturally seized upon Koevoet's aggressive reputation

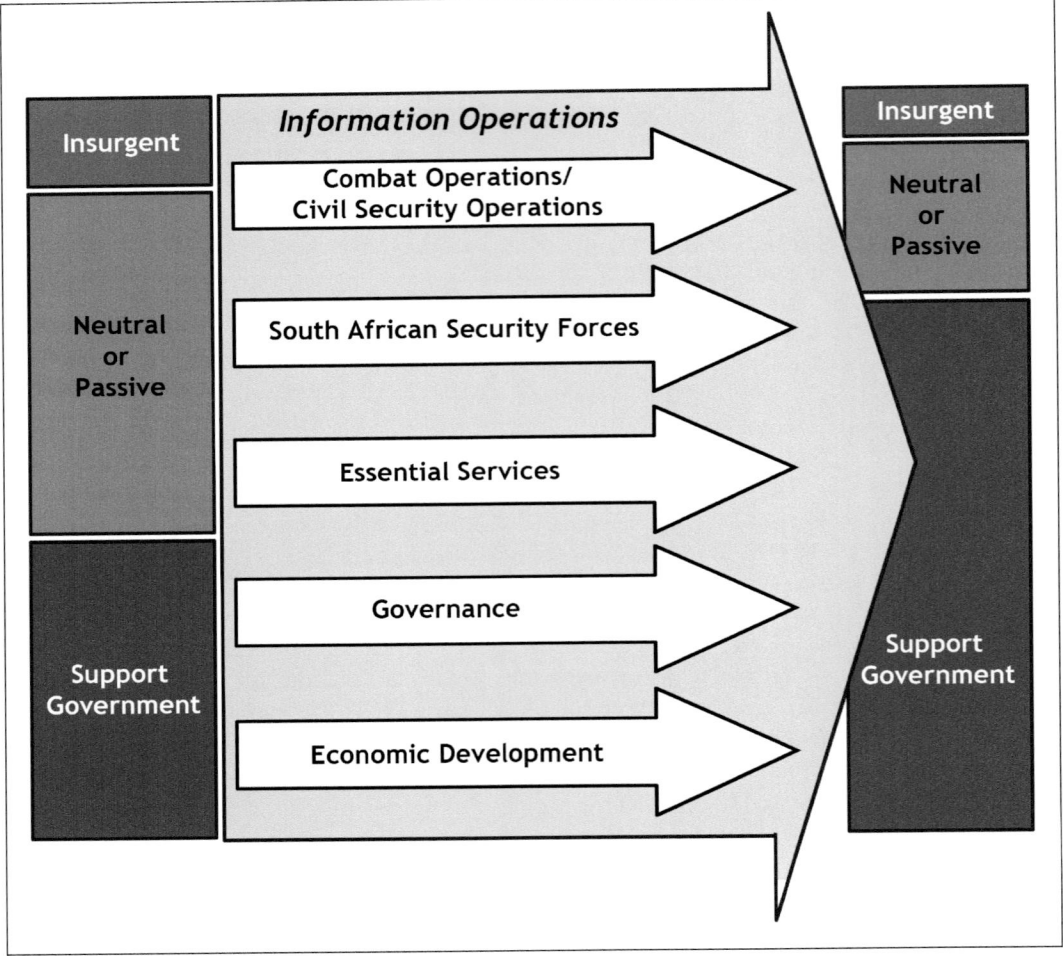

The South African LO Dashboard – Koevoet's role being to conduct civil security operations – policing – and when required, prosecute warfighting operations in partnership with the wider South African security force to neutralise SWAPO. (Diagram by Tom Cooper)

A patrolling call-sign mounted in its armoured Casspir complete with a dual re-barrelled 7.62mm Browning weapon fit. Discipline within Koevoet was strict and all members of Koevoet were held accountable for their actions. (Jim Hooper)

and accused Dreyer and his men of committing numerous, on the spot, extrajudicial killings and assassinations; of routinely mistreating prisoners and of using torture to elicit confessions. Certainly, excesses did occur and in Volume 2 of this two-part work, submissions to the Truth and Reconciliation Commission that detailed alleged Koevoet atrocities will be reviewed and assessed. As Kamongo remarked; 'A story did the rounds of one instance when a team commander stayed behind, alone in a Casspir parked in a deserted town. With him were nine FAPLA/SWAPO prisoners. He came back alone. He apparently did not let them go.'[13]

There were other well documented instances when members of Koevoet ran amok. One being Jonas Paulas, an Angolan tracker, who used an insurgent weapon to rob local stores, murder an elderly farmer and attempt to rape several girls. Detained by his former Koevoet colleagues, Paulas and his accomplice were handed over to the SWAPOL. Paulas was subsequently tried and hanged, his accomplice jailed.

There is no denying that Koevoet was a hard, focused and aggressive unit. It had to be, in order to prosecute the COIN mission, but when operating in Namibia, it was subject to the scrutiny of the SWAPOL and the strict code of conduct enforced within the unit by its experienced Ovambo NCOs;

> Next to the parade ground stands a man from one of the kraals which we have recently visited. One of the trackers of Casspit number 4 torched this man's mahongo field. The man duly identifies the policeman. Now we have to decide what to do. All the senior members black and white quickly form an impromptu disciplinary committee, with Lukas Koen as the chairman. It is decided that the whole team will have to contribute financially so mahongo meal can be purchased as compensation for this man. Each member will pay out R75; the total comes to R3,000 – a lot of money in Kavangoland, and for us especially. The money is soon collected and [we] send the Blesbok to buy 20 bags of mahnago meal as well as tinned food and other stuff. The local headman accompanies us as a witness when we deliver the food to the kraal.[14]

This adherence to some form of law and order did not apply to SWAPO and PLAN who exercised great brutality in terrorising the local population through murder, on the spot assassinations, kidnap, torture and sexual violence; insurgent methods and tactics that were illegal throughout, and for which, the insurgents chose to immerse themselves, as best possible, within the local population so as to evade both accountability and responsibility. This included concerted attempts to kill off-duty Koevoet trackers who were obvious prime targets for assassination. During the Koevoet's first five years to the end of 1984, more than 280 trackers were killed. Some at home where they lived off camp – as many chose to so with their families – or when travelling to and from their duty base.

Five years in and Koevoet was still having to address, daily, the challenge of identifying the insurgents. Certainly the call-signs had developed the practice of investigative policing to secure field intelligence and HUMINT; the tracker's local knowledge also added value as to who was who, but every day, the call-sign leaders and car commanders were having to determine who was potentially a SWAPO insurgent or a PLAN fighter. Who posed a threat and who, as a member of the local civil population, did not. This, in turn, led to the challenge of, when insurgents have been identified and a team is on the track, what level of lethal force is to be used and how is the potential for collateral damage – including the killing of innocent bystanders – minimised? Reducing the risk of such occurrences was a key Koevoet consideration in that the unnecessary killing of local people could aid SWAPO's intentions, by increasing resistance to the

South Africans. All of this suggests the exercise of proportionality in order to maintain the COIN momentum, balancing the need to defeat SWAPO through the application of the eight-part doctrinal construct, whilst also keeping the local population on side. In today's COIN practice, the issue of proportionality is a refined science – one that requires collateral damage to civil society infrastructures and the death of innocent bystanders to be minimised so as not to outweigh the security and military advantages of the COIN operation in question. Or rather, the obligation to reduce devastation and violence to a deemed acceptable level so that the COIN objectives can be achieved.

This science was much less defined in the early 1980s and Koevoet did kill innocent bystanders. One documented account notes that in pursuit of an insurgent, a Casspir was driven through a grass-hut and the family within simply run over. The daughter of the household was killed immediately and the mother, who was pregnant, sustained a broken pelvis. The insurgent was killed in the process.

But when faced with a determined insurgent enemy and with the immediacy of a contact, drawing reference from the British experience during the Malayan insurgency, Koevoet call-sign leaders were routinely faced with three warfighting options;

1. The commander may continue military operations in the area, limited only by the doctrines of necessity and proportionality, with the incidental death and injury to non-combatants that always attends such operations. While civilians may not be attacked as such, they have no immunity to military operations conducted against combatants in their midst.
2. The commander may suspend military operations in order to avoid the death of civilians. But this runs counter to the notion that nations pursue victory, that military forces seek to destroy the enemy, and that commanders will not allow their men to become the victims of operations conducted from a safe haven.
3. The commander may seek a way to segregate combatant from non-combatant, pursuing the former militarily and affording the latter protection.[15]

SWAPO was keen to portray Koevoet as out of control and reckless, and that its call-signs simply surged forward at every opportunity, to neutralise the insurgents with no thought for who as in the way; that its methods were brutal and inhumane. A specific example being the unit's detention of captured insurgents or others that were of interest to Dreyer and his leaders. Detention facilities were standard at each of the headquarter bases and, initially, Koevoet were at will to hold detainees without any legal representation or redress; though this was to be challenged later during the insurgency when the Namibian legal system ruled that all detainees were entitled to legal representation within a period of 30 days. SWAPO propaganda made great store of the torture meted out to the detainees including the use of sleep deprivation, exposure white noise, electric shock torture and more. Clearly, Koevoet was wishing to detain the 'persons of interest' to interrogate them for information as to SWAPO and PLAN activities.

The detention and interrogation of persons of interest is a standard COIN procedure and one that continues to be used today. Indeed, British military detentions during operations in Afghanistan were commonplace as the COIN effort sought to identify Taliban fighters and those that were supporting the insurgency, including those suspected of drug dealing. There, the coalition was legally empowered to hold detainees for up to 30 days. At the 24-day point, if they had not divulged any information and were still deemed to be of interest, they could be transferred to the Afghan National Directorate of Security (NSD) where they could be further detained and any interrogation continued.

For the call-sign leaders and car commanders, the urgency of a contact would require them to make quick and instant decisions. Separating the insurgent from the innocent bystander was always a challenge. (Jim Hooper)

As with the challenge of collateral damage, Koevoet would occasionally detain the innocent given that the intensity of operations, the invariable chaos of the pursuit and the confusion of the final action would certainly lead to snatch decisions as to who to capture and detain. Since the SWAPO insurgents and PLAN fighters operated in civilian clothes and looked to integrate into the local population by speaking their language and adopting cultural mannerisms, it was often difficult to separate those who might hold information from those who were bystanders. Yet the pressure upon Koevoet to secure information, so that the call-signs could move quickly to neutralise the insurgent threat, often meant quick decisions had to be made and that interrogations were robust. As a result, some of the detainees were quick to divulge whatever information or intelligence they held and, a number were obviously 'turned' to join Koevoet. When an innocent bystander is detained, there is the obvious risk that they will be radicalised in favour of the insurgency, particularly if they are subjected to torture and brutality. One of the challenges Koevoet had to address was how to maintain the policing/warfighting dynamic in a situation where large parts of the local population were voluntarily providing support to the Liberation War, as they saw it whilst, conversely, appearing to provide protection for the many, from the terrorist activities of a few. This was an especially complex issue for Koevoet given that it was suggested 'most of the Ovambos in eastern Ovamboland, particularly the [majority clan of the] Kwanyamas, were firmly on SWAPO's side. Satisfactory co-operation from the locals was rare and when it existed it had to be dealt with carefully.'[16]

This required Koevoet's leadership to be adept and quick to learn. Certainly, one of the elements of its success to 1984, had been its ability to adapt, improvise and overcome. Not just to the intransigence within the South African security services and the SADF in supporting the establishment of Koevoet in the first instance, but also the need to develop and retain a cultural understanding, as well as a more general understanding, of the societal, economic and political landscape of the affected country. This ability to read the cultural and tribal intricacies of the space in which it was operating, helped Koevoet develop a greater situational understanding of the insurgency and this informed the planning and execution of subsequent COIN operations. In turn, this required Dreyer to ensure Koevoet remained agile enough to respond to SWAPO's ever-changing threat and to its differing insurgent methodologies – terrorist attacks, infiltration, informational and political activities, the building of popular support across the local population.

In assessing the impact of Koevoet operations in 1984, SWAPO had certainly experienced setbacks. Operation Askari had led to significant losses in manpower and material, not to mention, morale. There was an increasing sense amongst the insurgents that the South Africans were proving a formidable enemy and SWAPO was having to pay for the 'protection' afforded by the MPLA by finding and equipping two infantry brigades for its war against UNITA. The Lusaka Accord also disrupted SWAPO's intentions, the JMC patrols denying SWAPO and PLAN access to its usual bases in southern Angola which then meant attempts were made to infiltrate into Namibia through Botswana. All of which failed.

Taking Stock – the Look Forward to 1989

From start-up in 1979 to the establishment of the first call-signs, the early development of doctrine, tactics, operational deployment and success, it was Dreyer's transformational leadership that led to Koevoet becoming a cohesive and, thereby, effective COIN asset. His emphasis on small unit identity, through maximising the power of Koevoet's insignia and its collective 'brand'; the emphasis on the thinking call-sign member who demonstrates self-discipline and utilises innovation to solve problems in the field; the store placed

A call-sign readies for operations. Its trackers ever alert for the next pursuit. (Jim Hooper)

on mutual respect and through such, the integration of black and white into one mission focused entity. Add to this, the Koevoet approach and methodology which Dreyer inspired, and which was further informed by the likes of de Kock and Conradie – this being the gathering of information through police work, the sifting and analysis of intelligence, the move to contact and action, with the projection of lethal and devastating force with which to neutralise the insurgents.

Through Dreyer's leadership and those of his senior commanders, the call-signs developed a skillset and capability that placed them well beyond the SAP COIN teams that had previously been operating in the 1970s in Ovamboland. Comprised of white policemen on rotation tours, these teams lacked local language skills and invariably struggled to gain the confidence of the local population. This hampered their effectiveness in countering SWAPO and contacts were rare as the SAP COIN teams failed to close with and engage SWAPO. Yet with the fledgling Koevoet teams, the SAP had a capability that was able to communicate with the indigenous peoples in their language of choice and, therefore, build the relationships that are essential for the gathering of intelligence and the delivery of an effective COIN strategy; utilising logical lines of operation to ensure optimisation of the COIN effort.

At the end of 1984, Koevoet stood on the edge of a further five years of operational existence. Five years that would see Koevoet amalgamated into the SWAPOL and be reconfigured as 'SWAPOL-TIN.' It would also see Koevoet grow in size to its peak utility of 42 call-signs and see the tempo of operations increase to a pace that was relentless, before dropping down to a point where; 'we were in charge of Ovamboland and the southern part of Angola and nobody would dare attack us.'[17]

But whilst Koevoet continued to be successful, towards 1988, the call-signs and the trackers within, began to notice the tide was turning with SWAPO and PLAN becoming ever more emboldened and assertive. The civil population was also turning to SWAPO; 'Normally SWAPO ran when we were closing in. This time it was different. On the way to the target areas where the insurgents had crossed the Angolan border we found SWAPO supporters dancing and singing in some of the kraals. Some of them shouted, "You won't be coming back, you are driving to your death."'[18]

There was a sense that the insurgency was coming to a head as the war-weary and stretched South Africans looked for some form of settlement and in May 1988, South African, Cuban and Angolan diplomats met in London for talks aimed at negotiating a cessation of hostilities.

In December 1988, South Africa committed to granting Namibia independence as per the detail of the Brazzaville Protocol. Mediated by the United States, the Protocol specified 1 April 1989 as the date that UN Security Council Resolution 435 was to be implemented, opening the way for Namibian independence. This and the resultant Tripartite Accord was to see the Cubans withdraw from Angola and the Angolan government affirm its intention to withdraw support and protection for PLAN. Two UN monitoring and peacekeeping missions, the United Nations Angola Verification Mission (UNAVEM) and the United Nations Transition Assistance Group (UNTAG) were to oversee preparations for independent elections and to ensure the return of PLAN and SADF units to their bases. This to include the demobilisation of paramilitary and auxiliary forces, including, of course, Koevoet. But this was not to be. In April 1989, PLAN reneged on the carefully negotiated ceasefire agreement and sought to move its forces into Namibia. Koevoet was tasked to respond, along with the SADF and SWATF, in what was to become known as Operation Merlyn or the Nine Day War.

During the period 1985 to 1989, Koevoet's effectiveness as a COIN capability grew exponentially. Volume 2 of this series documents the deployment of Koevoet as a force multiplier, releasing the SADF to focus on offensive combat operations in Angola, as opposed to having to divert resources to track insurgents in Namibia. It chronicles the unit's experience up to, and including, the Nine Day War, right through to its eventual disbandment and the demobilisation of all its operators in October 1989. A demobilisation process that would see the SAP abandon its black trackers to a dangerous and uncertain fate.

Bibliography

Angula, Oiva, *SWAPO Captive: A Comrade's Experience of Betrayal and Torture* (Cape Town, South Africa: Penguin Random House South Africa, 2018)

Cox, Sonny, 'Citizen Alert ZA, Koevoet veterans: "We don't give a damn for other people's wars," http://citizenalertzablogspotcom-tango.blogspot.com/2013/04/koevoet-veteranswe-dont-give-damn-for.html

de Kock, Eugene, and Gordin, Jeremy; *A Long Night's Damage: Working for the Apartheid State* (Saxonwold, South Africa: Contra Press, 1998)

Fowler, Barry; *SADF Border Base Layouts* (SADF Sentinel Projects, 2022) https://sadf.sentinelprojects.com/

Geldenhuys, Jannie, *At the Front: A General's Account Of South Africa's Border War* (Johannesburg, South Africa: Jonathan Ball, 2012)

Hamann, Hilton, *Days of the Generals: The untold story of South Africa's Apartheid-era Military Generals* (Alexandria, Virginia: Zebra Press, 2012)

Heitman, Helmoed-Romer, *Modern African Wars 3, South West Africa* (Oxford, England: Osprey, 1991)

Heitman, Helmoed-Romer, *South African Armed Forces* (Cape Town, South Africa: Buffalo Publications, 1990)

Herbstein, Denis and Evenson, John, *The Devils are Among Us: The War for Namibia* (London, England: Zed Press, 1989)

Hooper, Jim, *Black Vortex: One Man's Journey into Africa's Wars* (Warwick, England: Helion & Company, 2013)

Hooper, Jim, *Koevoet: Experiencing South Africa's Deadly Bush War* (Solihull, England: Helion & Company, 2013)

Jansen, Anemari, *Eugene de Kock: Assassin for the State* (Cape Town, South Africa: Tafelberg Publishers, 2015)

Kamongo, Sisingi and Bezuidenhout, Leon, *Shadows in the Sand, A Koevoet Tracker's Story of an Insurgency War* (Pinetown, South Africa: 30° South Publishers, 2011)

Katjavivi, Peter H., *A History of Resistance in Namibia* (Trenton, New Jersey: Africa World Press, 1990)

Leys, Colin and Saul, John S., *Namibia's Liberation Struggle: The Two-Edged Sword* (Athens, Ohio: Ohio University Press, 1995)

Nujoma, Sam, *Where Others Wavered* (Bedford, England: Panaf Books, 2001)

Pittaway, J., *Koevoet, The Men Speak* (Durban, South Africa: Dandy Agencies Publishing, 2016)

Scholtz, Leopold, 'The Namibian Border War: An Appraisal of the South African Strategy', *Scientia Militaria – South African Journal of Military Studies*, vol. 34 no. 1 (2006)

Scholtz, Leopold, *The SADF in the Border War 1966–1989* (Solihull, England: Helion & Company, 2013)

Seegers, A., *The Military in the Making of Modern South Africa* (London, England: Tauris Academic Studies, 1996)

Stapleton, Tim, 'Bush Tracking and Warfare in Late Twentieth-Century East and Southern Africa', *Historia* Volume 59: Issue 2 (2014), pp. 229–251

Stiff, Peter, *The Covert War: Koevoet Operations in Namibia, 1979–1989* (Johannesburg, South Africa: Galago Publishing, 2004)

Trooboof, Peter D. (ed.), *Law & Responsibility in Warfare: The Vietnam Experience* (Chapel Hill, North Carolina: University of North Carolina Press, 1976)

Vale, Peter, *Remembering Koevoet: How South Africa Has Come to Understand its Covert Military Operations in Namibia* (Washington, D.C.: Georgetown University Press, 2014)

van de Waag, Ian and Grundlingh, Albert, *In Different Times: The War for Southern Africa 1966–1989*, African Military Studies Vol 3 (Stellenbosch, South Africa: African Sun Media, 2019)

Venter, D., *South African Armoured Vehicles: A History of Innovation and Excellence* (Warwick, England: Helion & Company, 2020)

Visagie, Mike (2021), 'Koevoet Comments', E-mail (12 July 2021)

Notes

Acknowledgements
1. http://www.warinangola.com/

Chapter 1
1. Jim Hooper, *Koevoet: Experiencing South Africa's Deadly Bush War* (Warwick, England: Helion & Company, 2013), p. 37.
2. Peter Stiff, *The Covert War: Koevoet Operations in Namibia, 1979–1989* (Johannesburg, South Africa: Galago Publishing, 2004), p. 16.
3. Ian van de Waag, and Albert Grundlingh, *In Different Times: The War for Southern Africa 1966–1989*, African Military Studies Vol 3 (Stellenbosch, South Africa: African Sun Media, 2019), p. 31.
4. van de Waag and Grundlingh, *In Different Times*, p. 32.
5. van de Waag and Grundlingh, *In Different Times*, p. 33.
6. Stiff, *The Covert War*, p. 27.
7. A. Seegers, *The Military in the Making of Modern South Africa* (London, England: Tauris Academic Studies, 1996), p. 137.
8. Stiff, *The Covert War*, p. 30.
9. Seegers, *The Military in the Making of Modern South Africa*, p. 138.
10. Tim Stapleton, 'Bush Tracking and Warfare in Late Twentieth-Century East and Southern Africa', *Historia*, 59:2 (2014), p. 243.
11. Stiff, *The Covert War*, p. 48.
12. Stiff, *The Covert War*, p. 50.
13. Stapleton, 'Bush Tracking and Warfare in Late Twentieth-Century East and Southern Africa', *Historia*, p. 244.

Chapter 2
1. Helmoed-Romer Heitman, *Modern African Wars 3, South West Africa* (Oxford, England: Osprey, 1991), p. 17.
2. Anemari Jansen, *Eugene de Kock: Assassin for the State* (Cape Town, South Africa: Tafelberg Publishers, 2015), p. 42.
3. Jansen, *Eugene de Kock*, p. 50.
4. Jansen, *Eugene de Kock*, p. 61.
5. Jansen, *Eugene de Kock*, p. 73.
6. van de Waag and Grundlingh, *In Different Times*, p. 36.
7. Jansen, *Eugene de Kock*, p. 73.
8. Jansen, *Eugene de Kock*, p. 78.

Chapter 3
1. J. Pittaway, *Koevoet, The Men Speak* (Durban, South Africa: Dandy Agencies, 2016), p. 239.
2. Jansen, *Eugene de Kock*, p. 94.
3. Jansen, *Eugene de Kock*, p. 94.
4. Pittaway, *Koevoet, The Men Speak*, p. 240.
5. Sam Nujoma, *Where Others Wavered* (Bedford, England: Panaf Books, 2001), pp. 315–316.

6. Pittaway, *Koevoet, The Men Speak*, p. 254.
7. Seegers, *The Military in the Making of Modern South Africa*, p. 225.
8. Jansen, *Eugene de Kock*, p. 99.
9. Hooper, *Koevoet: Experiencing South Africa's Deadly Bush War*, p. 116.
10. Jansen, *Eugene de Kock*, p. 99.
11. Pittaway, *Koevoet, The Men Speak*, p. 198.
12. Pittaway, *Koevoet, The Men Speak*, p. 206.
13. Stiff, *The Covert War*, p. 62.
14. Stiff, *The Covert War*, p. 72.
15. Hooper, *Koevoet: Experiencing South Africa's Deadly Bush War*, p. 117.
16. Hooper, *Koevoet: Experiencing South Africa's Deadly Bush War*, p. 117.

Chapter 4
1. Hooper, *Koevoet: Experiencing South Africa's Deadly Bush War*, p. 110.
2. Visagie, Mike (2021), 'Koevoet Comments', E-mail (12 July 2021).
3. Sisingi Kamongo and Leon Bezuidenhout, *Shadows in the Sand, A Koevoet Tracker's Story of an Insurgency War* (Pinetown, South Africa: 30° South Publishers, 2011), p. 37.
4. Kamongo and Bezuidenhout, *Shadows in the Sand*, p. 37.
5. D. Venter, *South African Armoured Vehicles: A History of Innovation and Excellence* (Warwick, England: Helion & Company, 2020), p. 31.
6. Venter, *South African Armoured Vehicles*, p. 31.
7. Stiff, *The Covert War*, p. 73.
8. Pittaway, *Koevoet, The Men Speak*, p. 268.
9. Pittaway, *Koevoet, The Men Speak*, p. 298.
10. Visagie, E-mail.
11. Pittaway, *Koevoet, The Men Speak*, p. 268.
12. Pittaway, *Koevoet, The Men Speak*, p. 269.
13. Kamongo and Bezuidenhout, *Shadows in the Sand*, p. 139.
14. Stiff, *The Covert War*, p. 311.

Chapter 5
1. Leopold Scholtz, *The SADF in the Border War 1966–1989* (Warwick, England: Helion & Company, 2013), p. 199.
2. Helmoed-Romer Heitman, *South African Armed Forces* (Cape Town, South Africa: Buffalo Publications, 1990), p. 113.
3. Hooper, *Koevoet: Experiencing South Africa's Deadly Bush War*, p. 112.
4. Pittaway, *Koevoet, The Men Speak*, p. 331.
5. Visagie, E-mail.
6. Pittaway, *Koevoet, The Men Speak*, p. 293.
7. Hooper, *Koevoet: Experiencing South Africa's Deadly Bush War*, p. 115.
8. Stiff, *The Covert War*, p. 149.
9. Peter H. Katjavivi, *A History of Resistance in Namibia* (London: Africa World Press, 1990), p. 88.
10. Katjavivi, *A History of Resistance in Namibia*, p. 88.
11. Pittaway, *Koevoet, The Men Speak*, p. 261.
12. Kamongo and Bezuidenhout, *Shadows in the Sand*, p. 106.
13. Denis Herbstein and John Evenson, *The Devils are Among Us: The War for Namibia* (London, England: Zed Press, 1989), p. 71.
14. Oiva Angula, *SWAPO Captive: A Comrade's Experience of Betrayal and Torture* (Cape Town, South Africa: Penguin Random House South Africa, 2018), p. 87.
15. Peter Vale, *Remembering Koevoet: How South Africa Has Come to Understand its Covert Military Operations in Namibia* (Washington, D.C.: Georgetown University Press, 2014), p. 50.
16. Bezuidenhout and Kamongo, *Shadows in the Sand*, p. 60.

Chapter 6
1. Stiff, *The Covert War*, p. 156.
2. Stiff, *The Covert War*, p. 164.
3. Stiff, *The Covert War*, p. 172.

Chapter 7
1. Pittaway, *Koevoet, The Men Speak*, p. 261.
2. Visagie, E-mail.
3. Visagie, E-mail.
4. Visagie, E-mail.
5. Stiff, *The Covert War*, p. 181.
6. Stiff, *The Covert War*, p. 178.
7. Visagie, E-mail.
8. Visagie, E-mail.
9. Visagie, E-mail.
10. Visagie, E-mail.
11. Stapleton, 'Bush Tracking and Warfare in Late Twentieth-Century East and Southern Africa', *Historia*, p. 246.
12. Stiff, *The Covert War*, p. 187.
13. Pittaway, *Koevoet, The Men Speak*, p. 300.
14. Visagie, E-mail.
15. Visagie, E-mail.
16. Pittaway, *Koevoet, The Men Speak*, p. 304.
17. Visagie, E-mail.
18. Stiff, *The Covert War*, p. 200.
19. Pittaway, *Koevoet, The Men Speak*, p. 420.

Chapter 8
1. Bezuidenhout and Kamongo, *Shadows in the Sand*, p. 48.
2. Bezuidenhout and Kamongo, *Shadows in the Sand*, p. 95.
3. Pittaway, *Koevoet, The Men Speak*, p. 450.
4. Pittaway, *Koevoet, The Men Speak*, p. 318.
5. Pittaway, *Koevoet, The Men Speak*, p. 401.
6. Stiff, *The Covert War*, p. 212.
7. Hooper, *Koevoet: Experiencing South Africa's Deadly Bush War*, p. 77.
8. Bezuidenhout and Kamongo, *Shadows in the Sand*, p. 49.
9. Hooper, *Koevoet: Experiencing South Africa's Deadly Bush War*, p. 173.
10. Bezuidenhout and Kamongo, *Shadows in the Sand*, p. 35.
11. Hooper, *Koevoet: Experiencing South Africa's Deadly Bush War*, p. 161.
12. Scholtz, *The SADF in the Border War 1966–1989*, p. 211.
13. Kamongo and Bezuidenhout, *Shadows in the Sand*, p. 126.
14. Kamongo and Bezuidenhout, *Shadows in the Sand*, p. 103.
15. Peter D. Trooboof (ed.), *Law & Responsibility in Warfare: The Vietnam Experience* (Chapel Hill, North Carolina: University of North Carolina Press, 1976), p. 58.
16. Leopold Scholtz, 'The Namibian Border War: An Appraisal of the South African Strategy', *Scientia Militaria – South African Journal of Military Studies*, vol. 34 no. 1 (2006), p. 411.
17. Pittaway, *Koevoet, The Men Speak*, p. 271.
18. Bezuidenhout and Kamongo, *Shadows in the Sand*, p. 190.

About the Author

Steve Crump has served in the UK armed forces and has worked at senior level in a number of humanitarian, development and global health organisations, including the International Committee of the Red Cross (ICRC) and the Mines Advisory Group (MAG). In 1997 and as Programme Co-ordinator for the MAG mine action programme in Angola, he worked to oversee a number of clearance operations in Moxico, Cunene and Cuando Cubango, aimed at clearing the legacy of the Namibian War of Independence; namely landmines and unexploded ordnance. He also worked to support MAG's Namibian assessment mission which saw MAG collaborate with the Explosives Inspectorate of the Namibian Police to ascertain the potential for joint clearance work in northern Namibia. Through his experiences in Angola and Namibia, Steve became interested in the South African counter-insurgency effort and the result is this two-volume set.